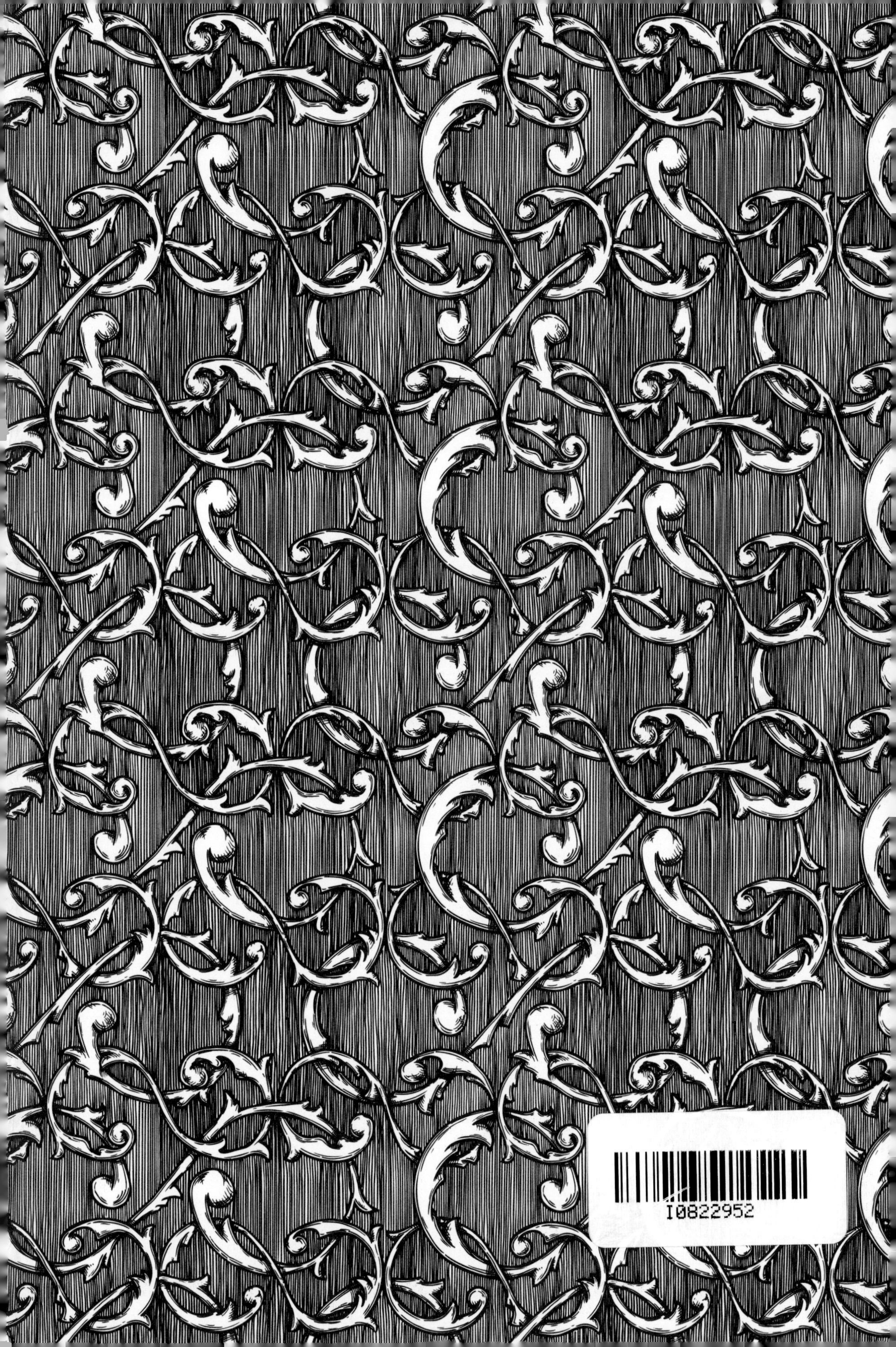
I0822952

Published by Familius LLC, www.familius.com
PO Box 1130, Sanger, CA 93657

Familius books are available at special discounts for bulk purchases, whether for sales promotions or for family or corporate use. For more information, contact Familius Sales at orders@familius.com.

Library of Congress Control Number: 2026935700

Print ISBN 9798893961874
Ebook ISBN 9798893962123

Printed in China

Edited by Gretchen Picklesimer Kinney
Cover and book design by Brooke Jorden
Photo Credit: Randhy Rodriguez

10 9 8 7 6 5 4 3 2 1

First Edition

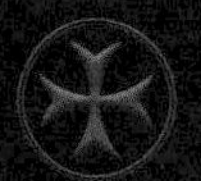

Alphabet of Oddities

A GOTHIC BESTIARY

Ronald Porcelli

"To represent terrible and questionable things is, in itself, the sign of an instinct of power and magnificence in the artist; he doesn't fear them."

—Friedrich Nietzsche, *The Will to Power*

Life is a series of stepping stones. Stepping stones on a path that leads us on a personal journey across rough roads and smooth. A path with twists and turns both wonderful and horrible. A very personal path that we tread, searching . . . Searching for what? Our bliss.

My bliss has always been the arts—viewing and creating. The seed for this book was originally planted in my head over forty years ago, while working in the bookroom in Richmond Hill High School in Queens. As I was sitting around after helping Mr. Banilower stack the books, the lines came to my head: "A is for Adzooks that walk with no head, B is for Boozoins that feed on the dead."

I thought to myself, "What great lines!" It would be interesting to write a book of letters, where each letter is represented by a weird, whimsical creature. In the following days, I jotted down some more lines, but in time I put aside the project and misplaced the additional lines, but remembered the first two lines as if they were inscribed in my brain.

After high school and college at SVA, I made the grave mistake of allowing the world to devour me. I was caught up in making a living and didn't put anywhere near as much time in my artwork or writing.

About ten years after high school, I published an illustrated edition of the works of Poe, The *Essential Poe: Tales of Horror and Mystery*, that contained twenty-seven of my illustrations for various Edgar Allen Poe stories. The book did not sell well, but it put the bug in my head to return to the right road, the world that will take me to my personal bliss: the world of illustration.

After *The Essential Poe* was published, I continued to hit the proverbial time clock, but with a fever to illustrate that was truly overwhelming.

The next project I decided to do was illustrate the oldest vampire novel ever written in the English language (*Varney the Vampire* by James Rymer, originally published in 1847). It was a massive project taking three years of intense work. But the book, an almost nine-hundred page tome, was so large it couldn't get off the ground. No publisher wanted to handle so huge a project written by an author whose name is forgotten to the ages and illustrated by a fairly unknown artist.

This was all very discouraging, especially with all the work put into the art, that I hardly worked on much art (except a few small projects here and there) for the next few years. And then along came Caryl Ehrlich.

Caryl put out an ad for an artist to illustrate a line of greeting cards that would promote her self-help program. I brought my portfolio to her and she fell in love with my black-and-white illustrations, which reminded her of nineteenth-century artists such as Doré, Phiz, and Tenniel—artists who have always been inspirations to me.

Now we approach the cobblestone path that leads directly to this book.

In 2000, Caryl asked me to paint illustrations on a modern chair she has in her apartment. I had never done such a project before. I really didn't think my artwork would be suited to this job, and yet, I felt bad just saying no to Caryl because she had been very kind and helpful to me.

I had the idea to send her an illustrated poem about why I couldn't work on this project. The poem became "The Chair," and Caryl loved it. (She tells me she had every drawing framed and they are hanging on her office wall.)

“The Chair” was such a big hit that it got me thinking of my book of letters for the first time in years. I immediately completed the poem and for the next few years worked on the illustrations.

All my life I have been enthralled by the quality of the illustrations by such nineteenth-century artists as I have mentioned. And I have always attempted to reach the heights of their greatness. Whether I have lived up to these expectations, you be the judge.

So take my hand. We shall jump down the proverbial rabbit hole together. But be warned, Alice! This ain’t no Wonderland.

A is for Adzooks that walk with no head.

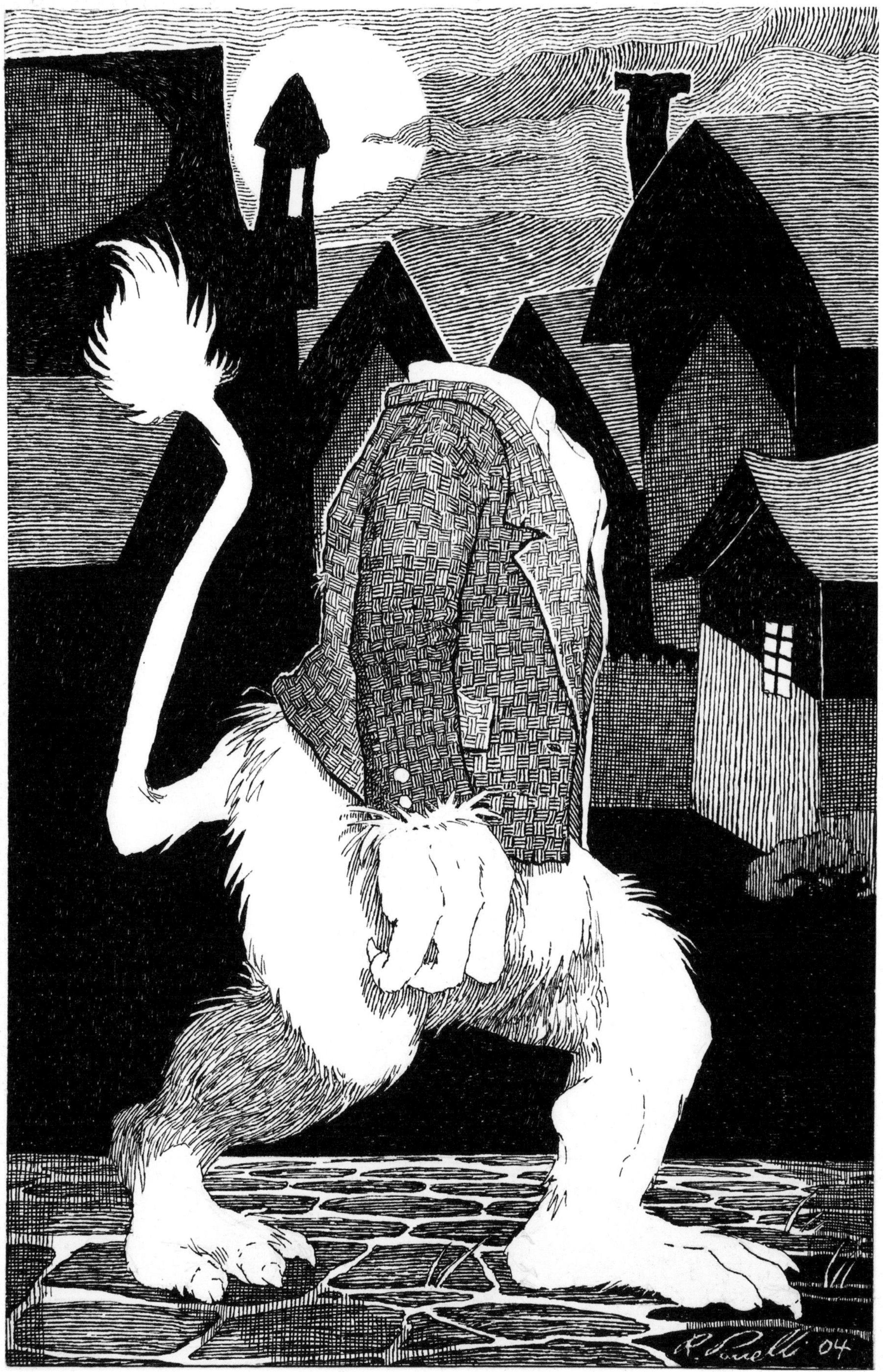

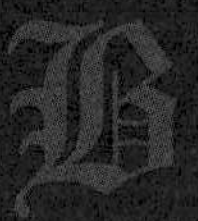 is for Boozoins that feed on the dead.

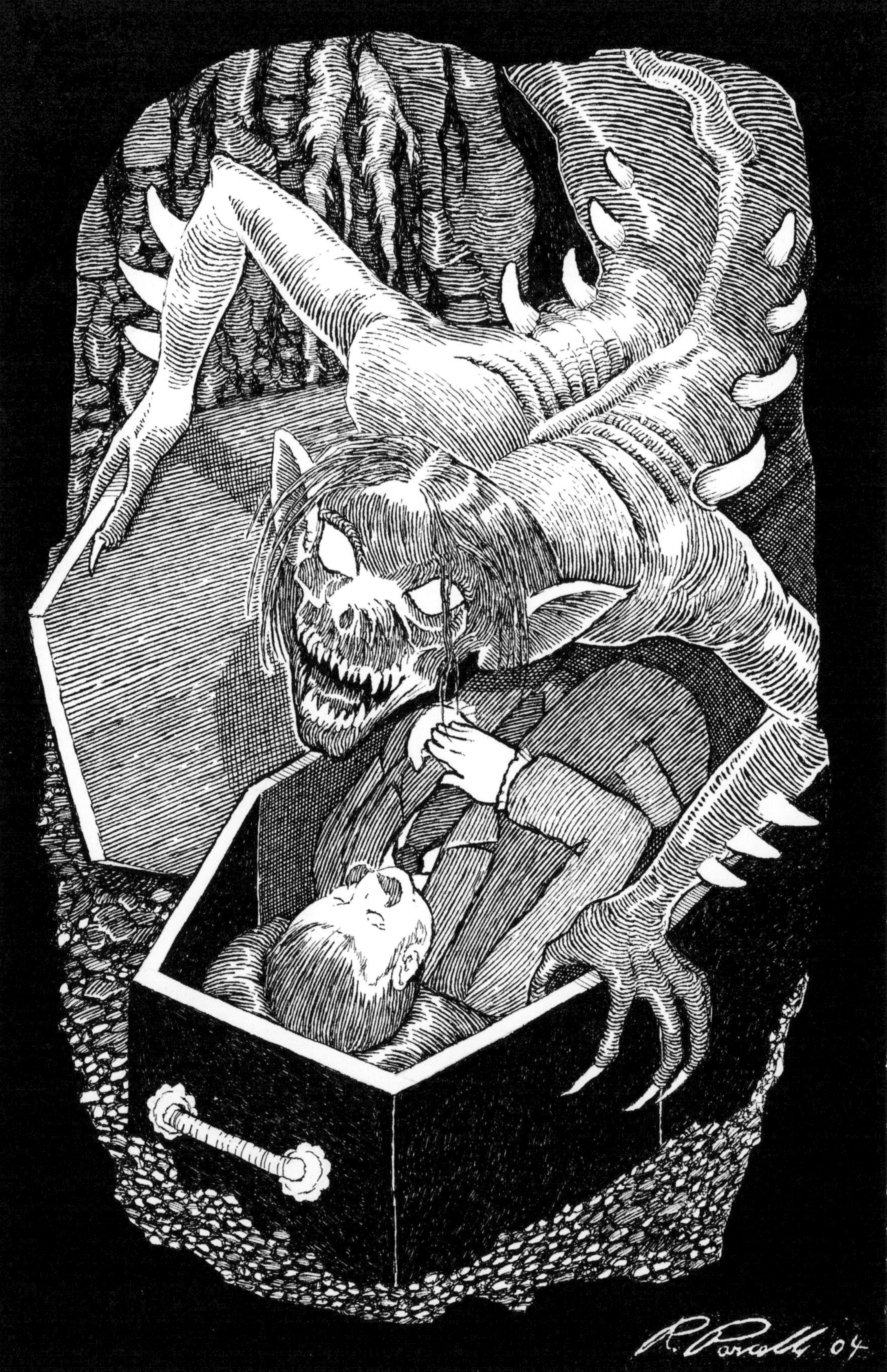

C is for Crackings—sweet, they just look gruff.

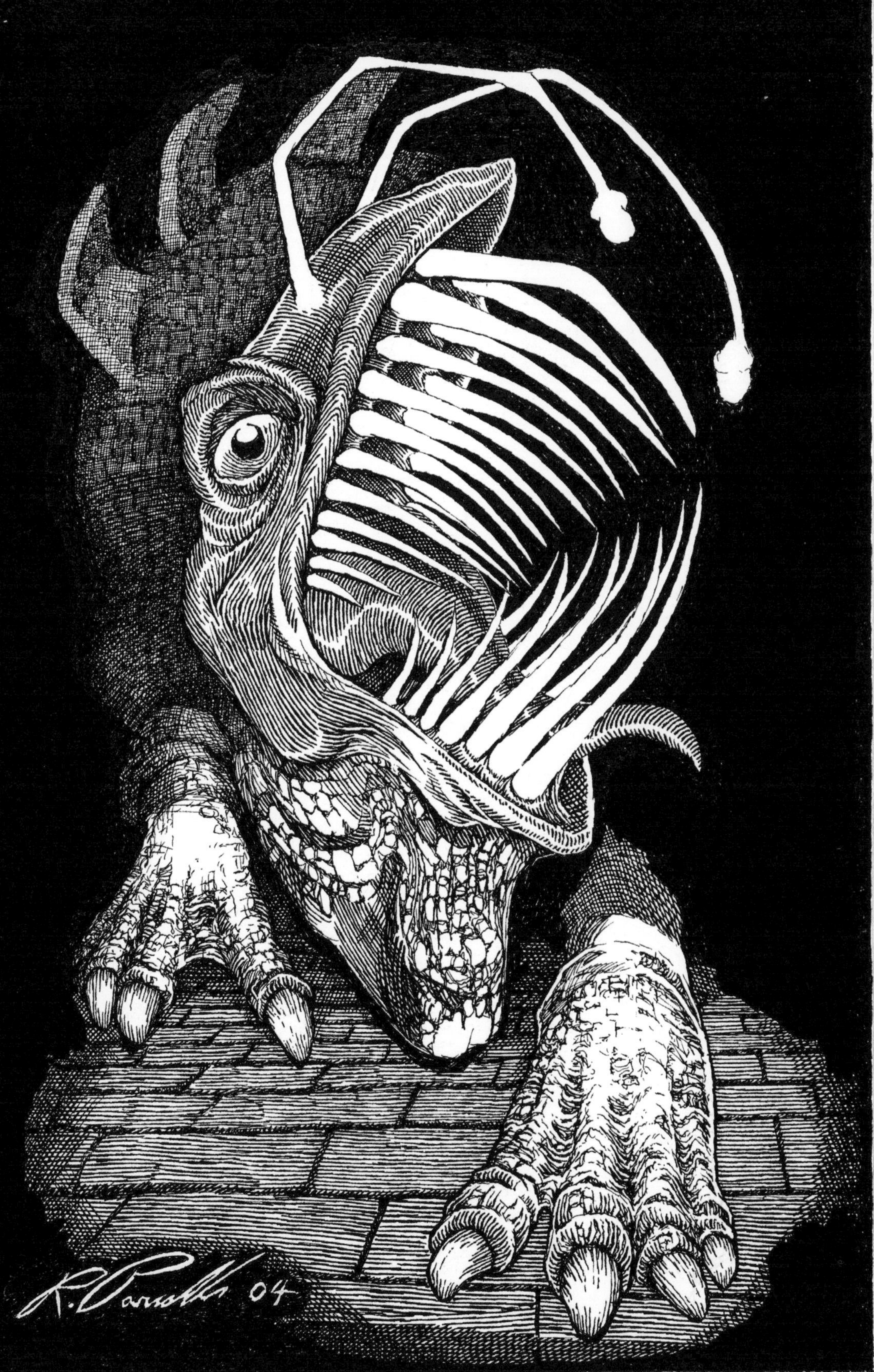

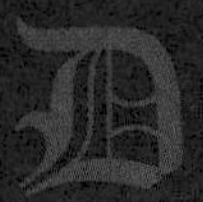 is for Dankies, tiny as dandruff.

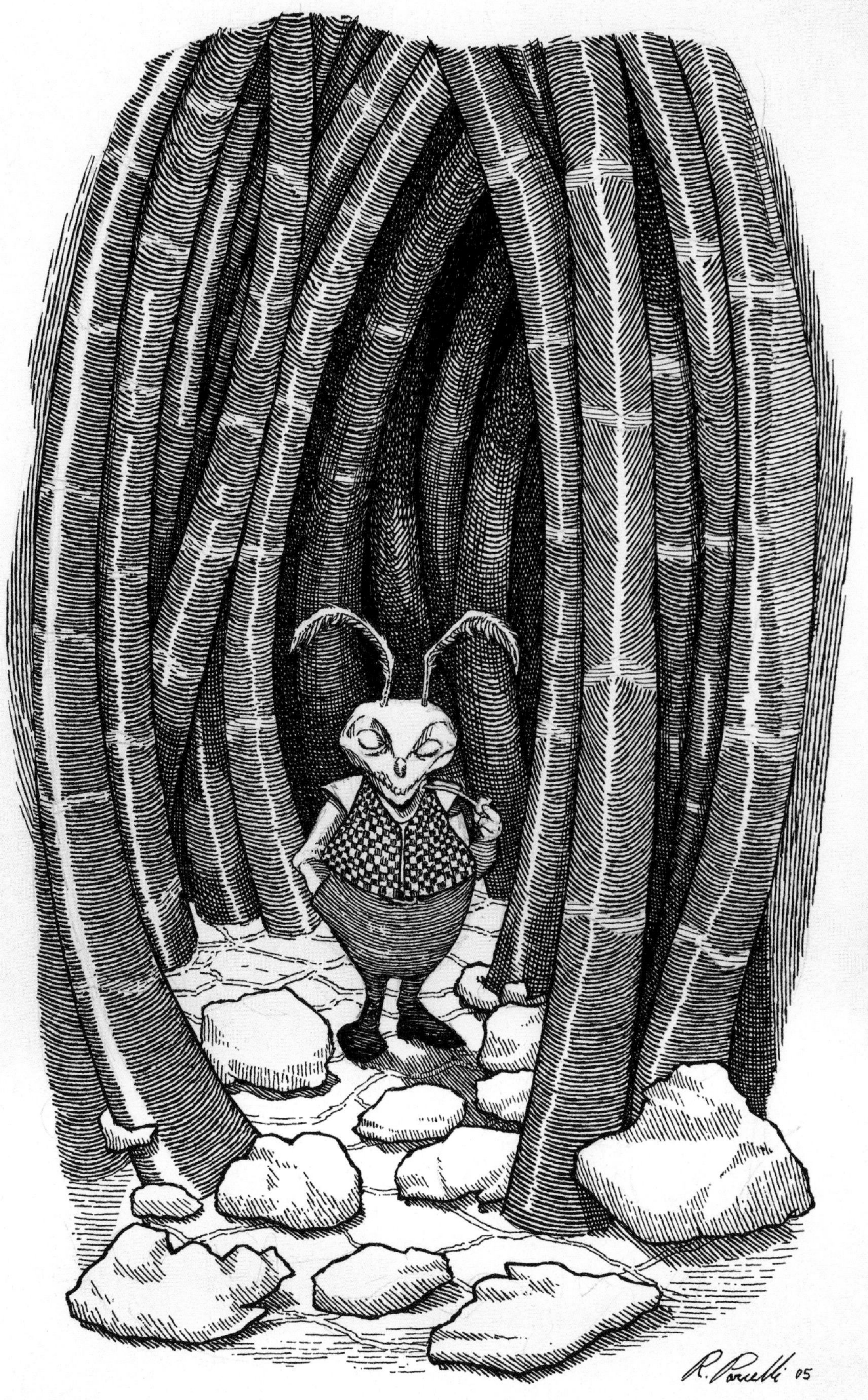

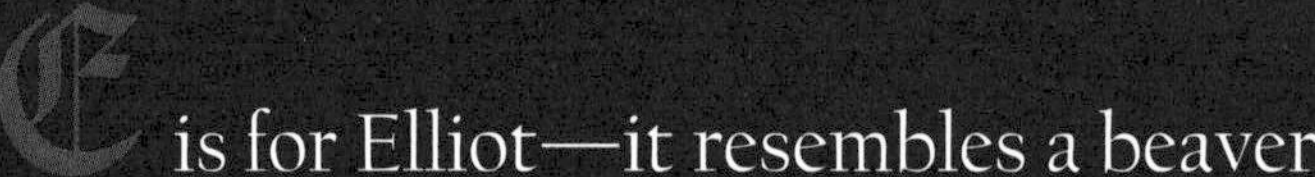

E is for Elliot—it resembles a beaver.

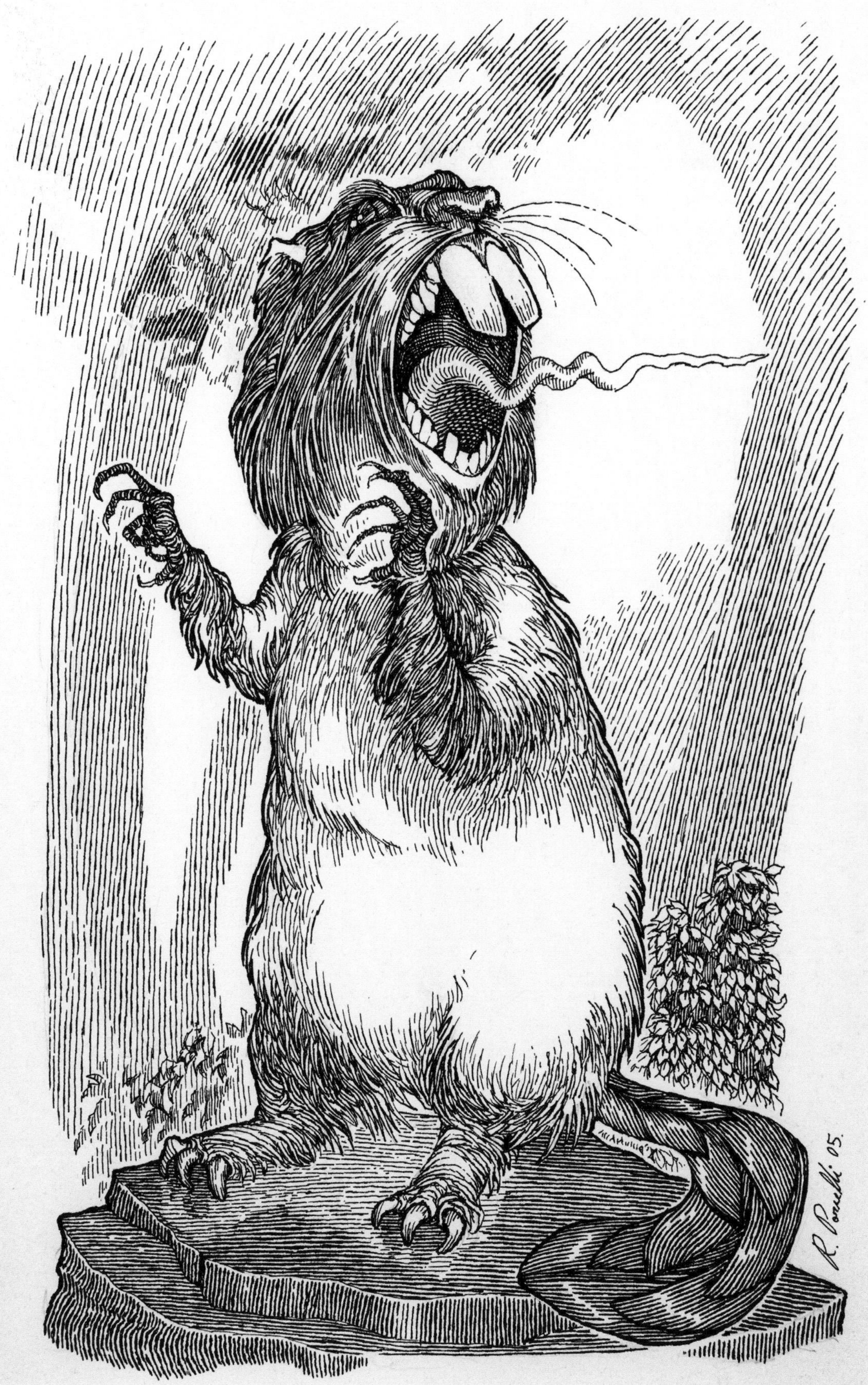
R. Porcelli 05.

F is for Fxchopxtinks—I can't pronounce it either.

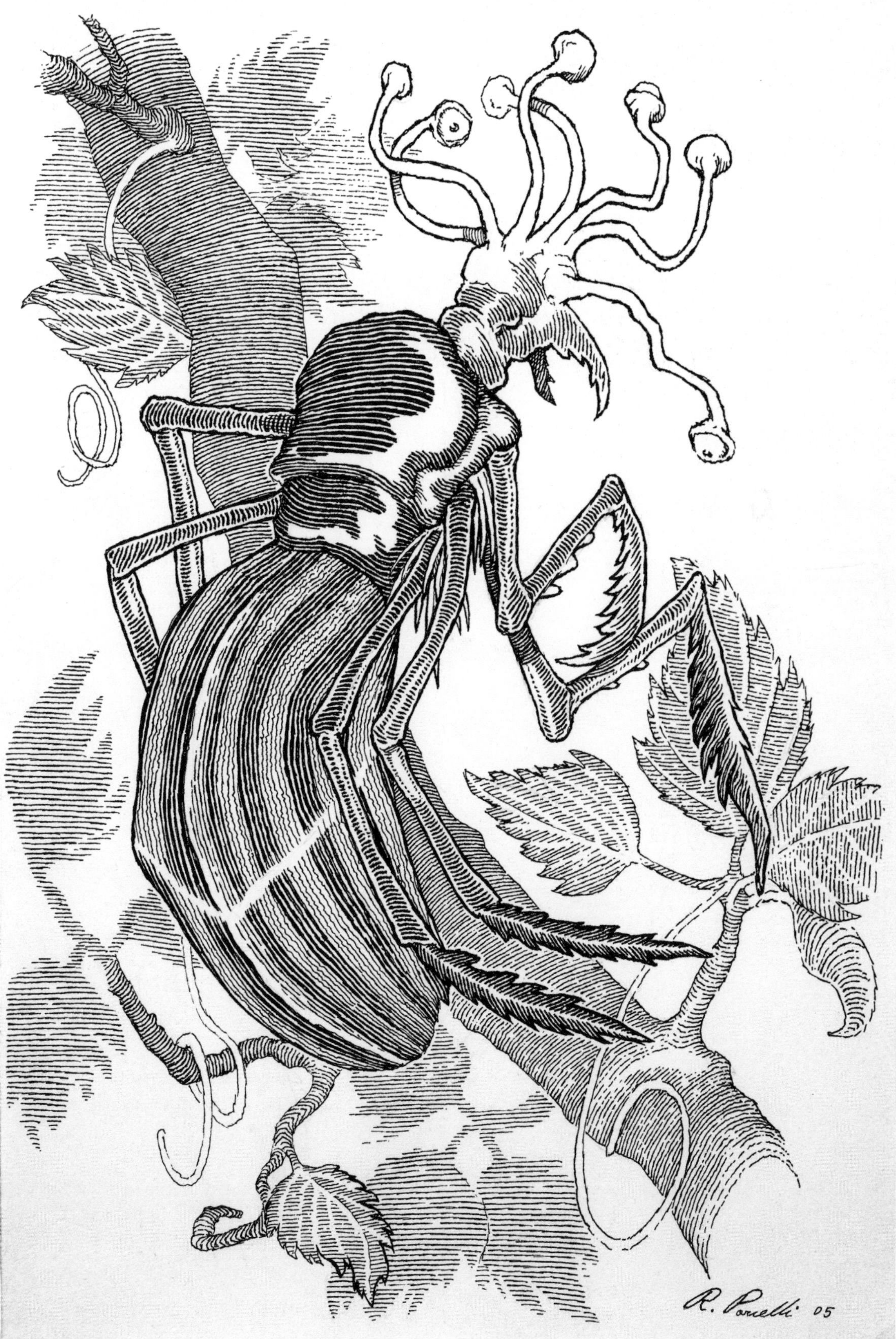
R. Porcelli 05

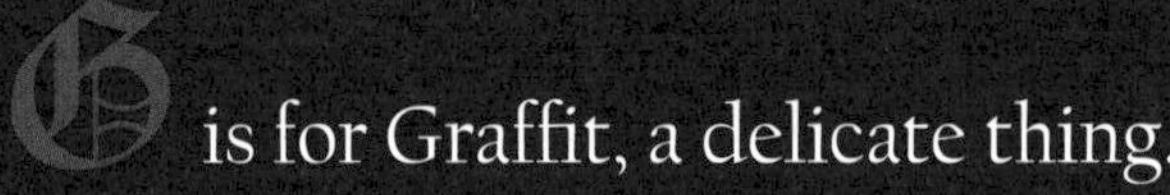

G is for Graffit, a delicate thing.

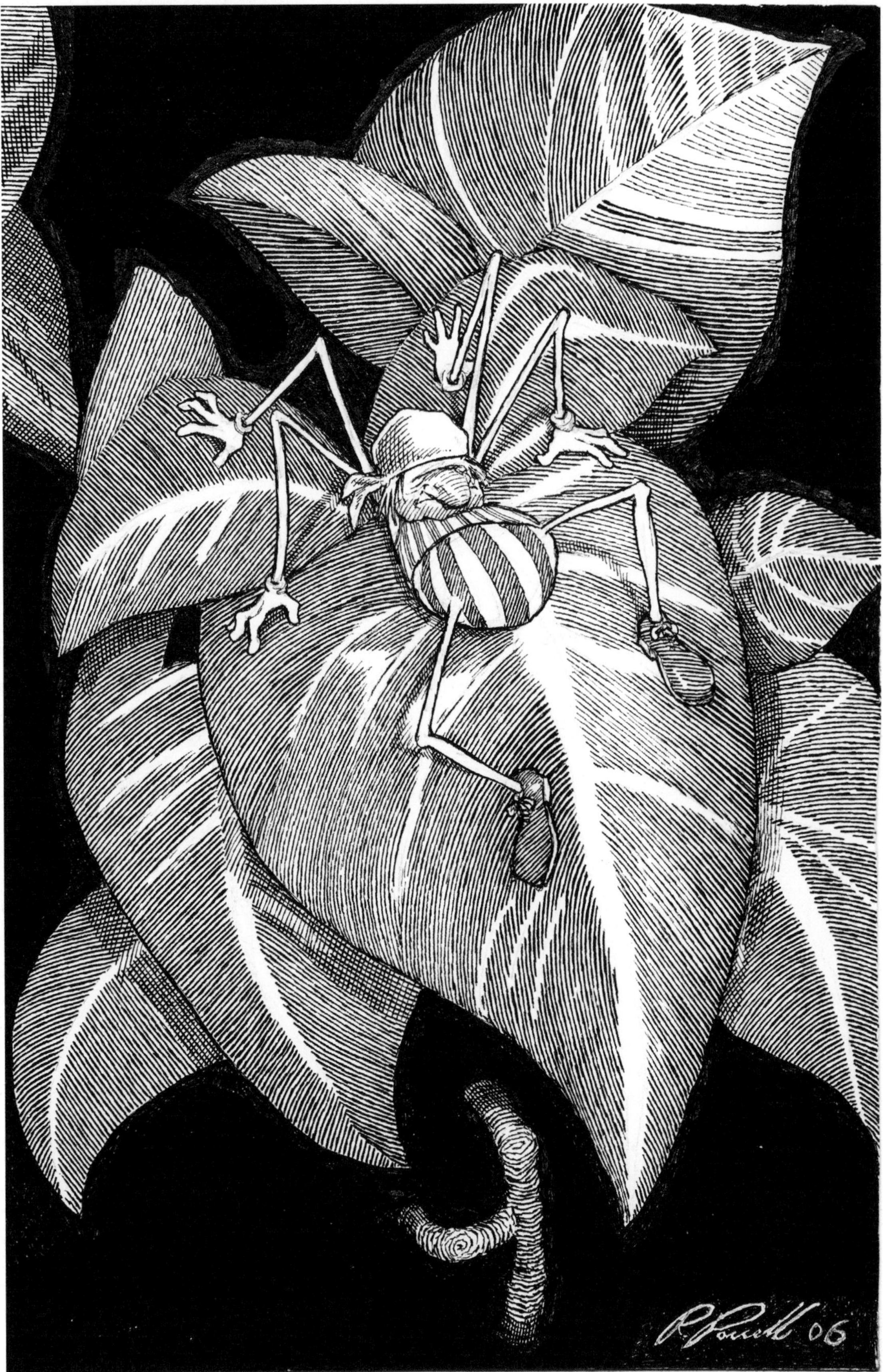

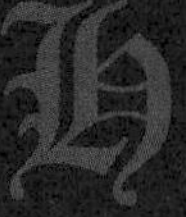 is for Hiss-rocs, only one head can sing.

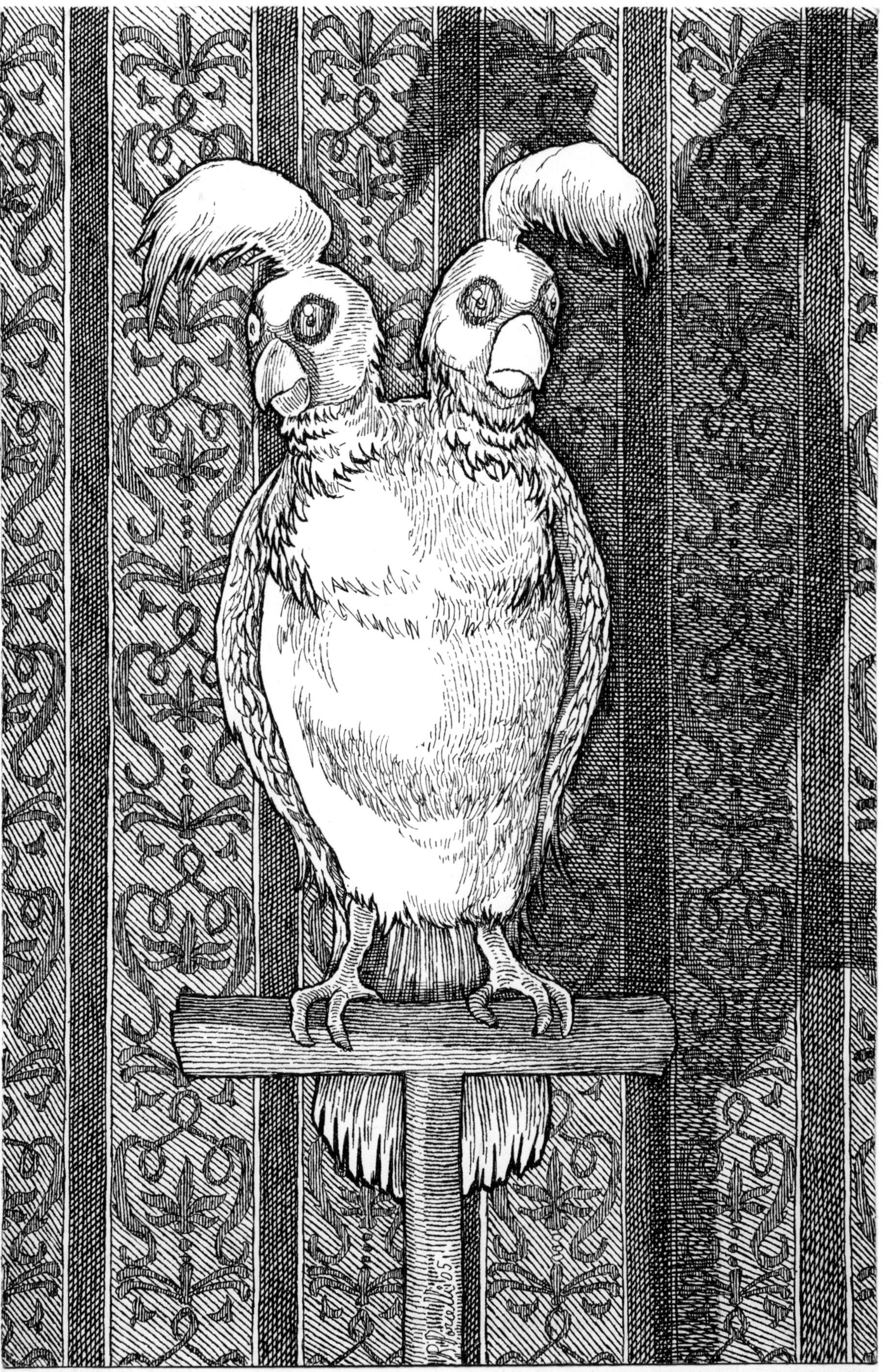

I is for Ice-wolf—it's rabbit it's after.

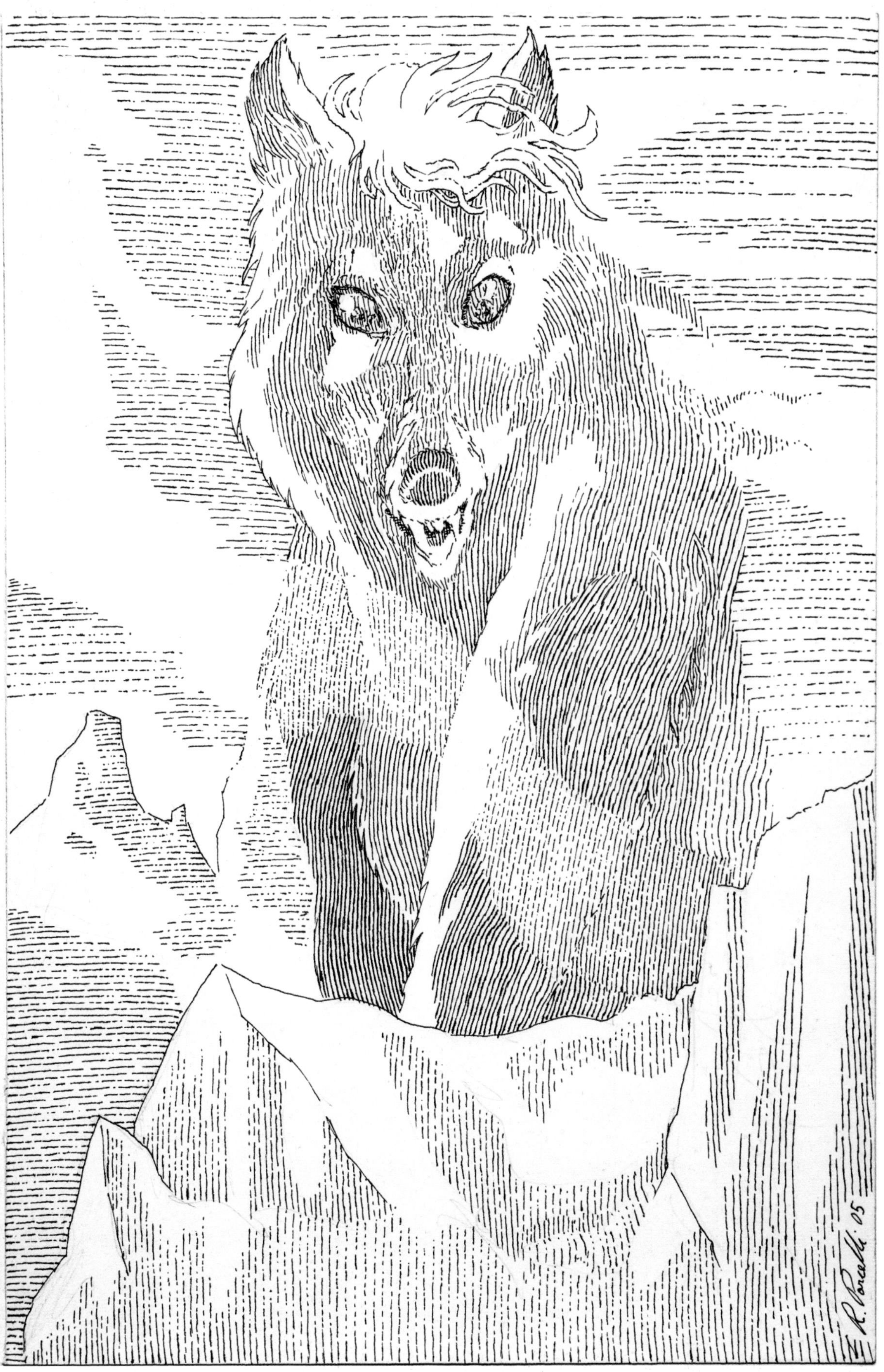

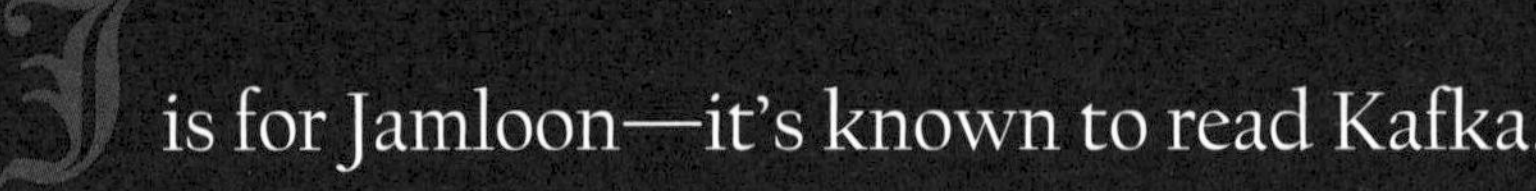

J is for Jamloon—it's known to read Kafka.

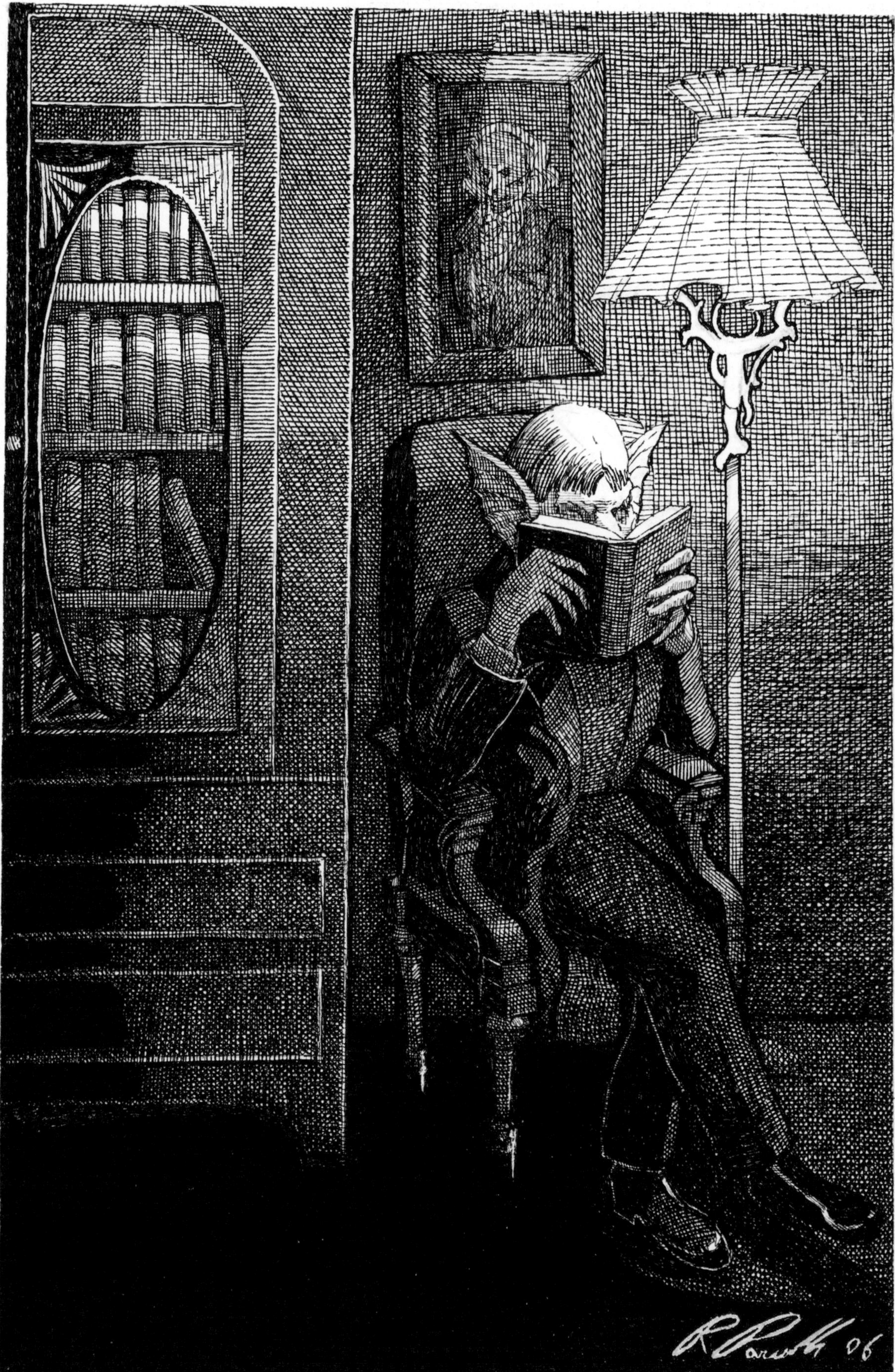

K is for Kraffish, a fish out of water.

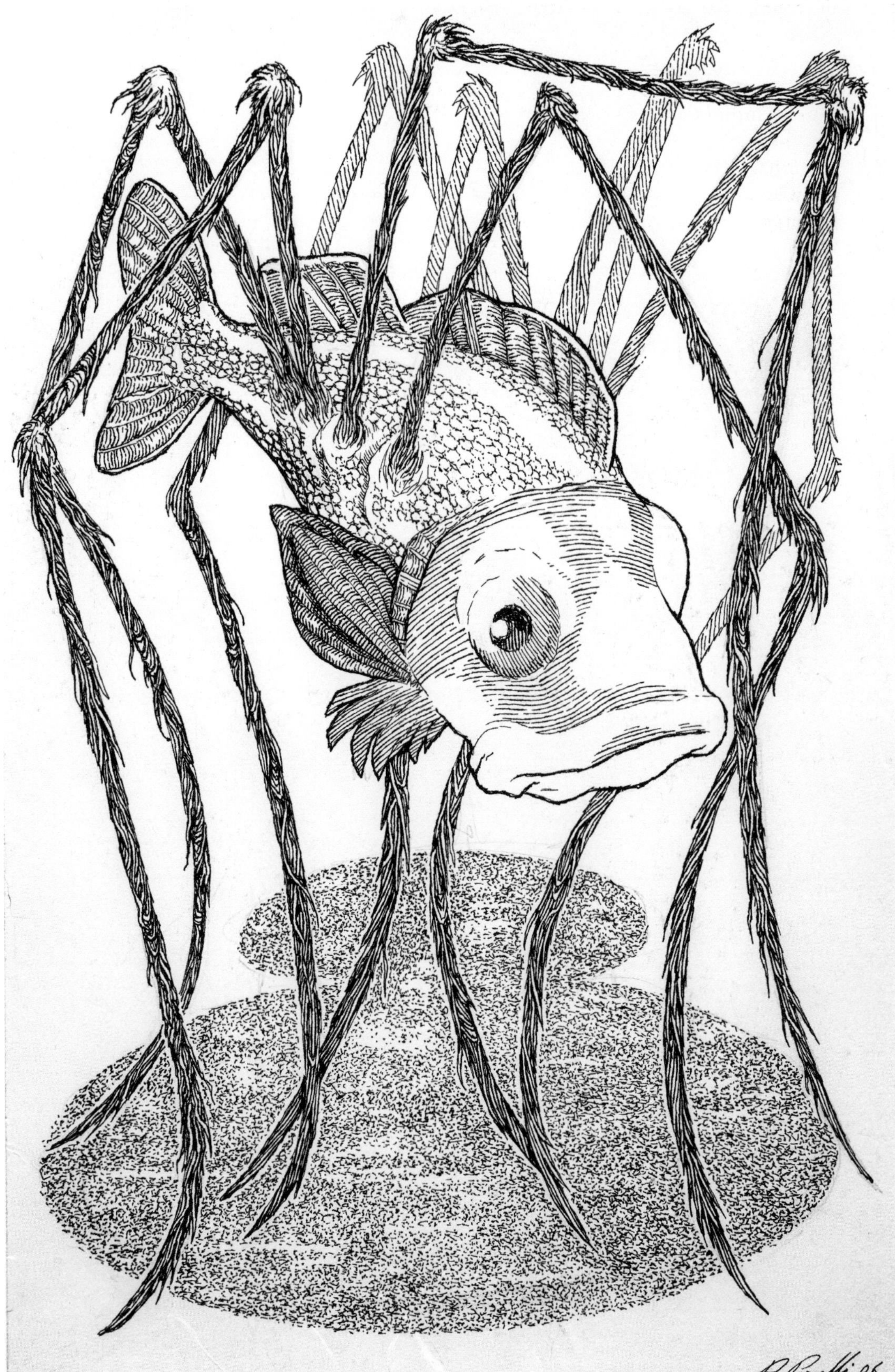

L is for Loomis—they don't pray, but ought'a.

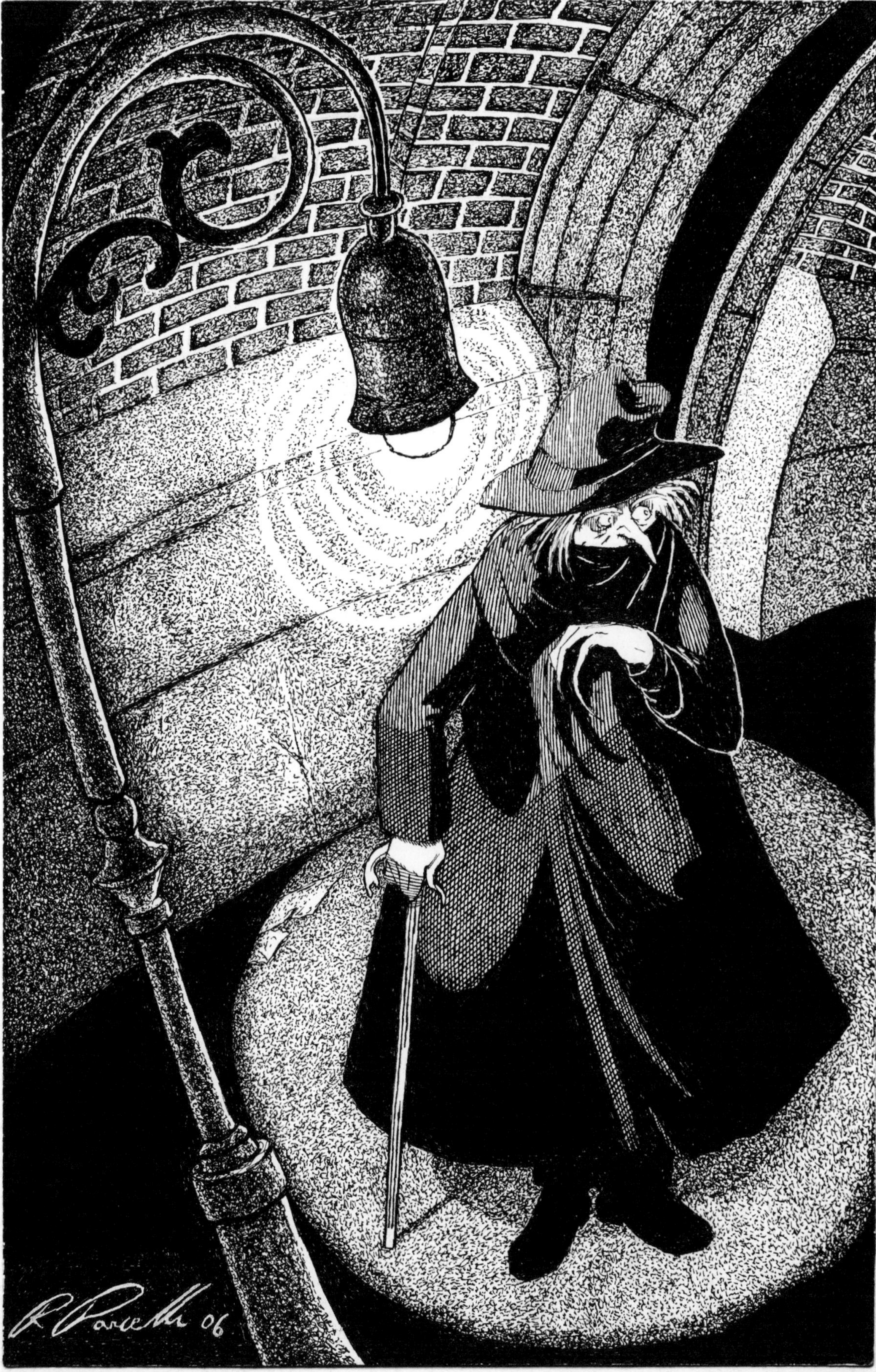

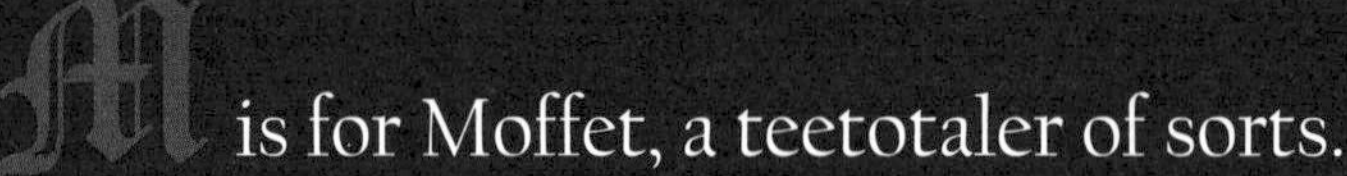

M is for Moffet, a teetotaler of sorts.

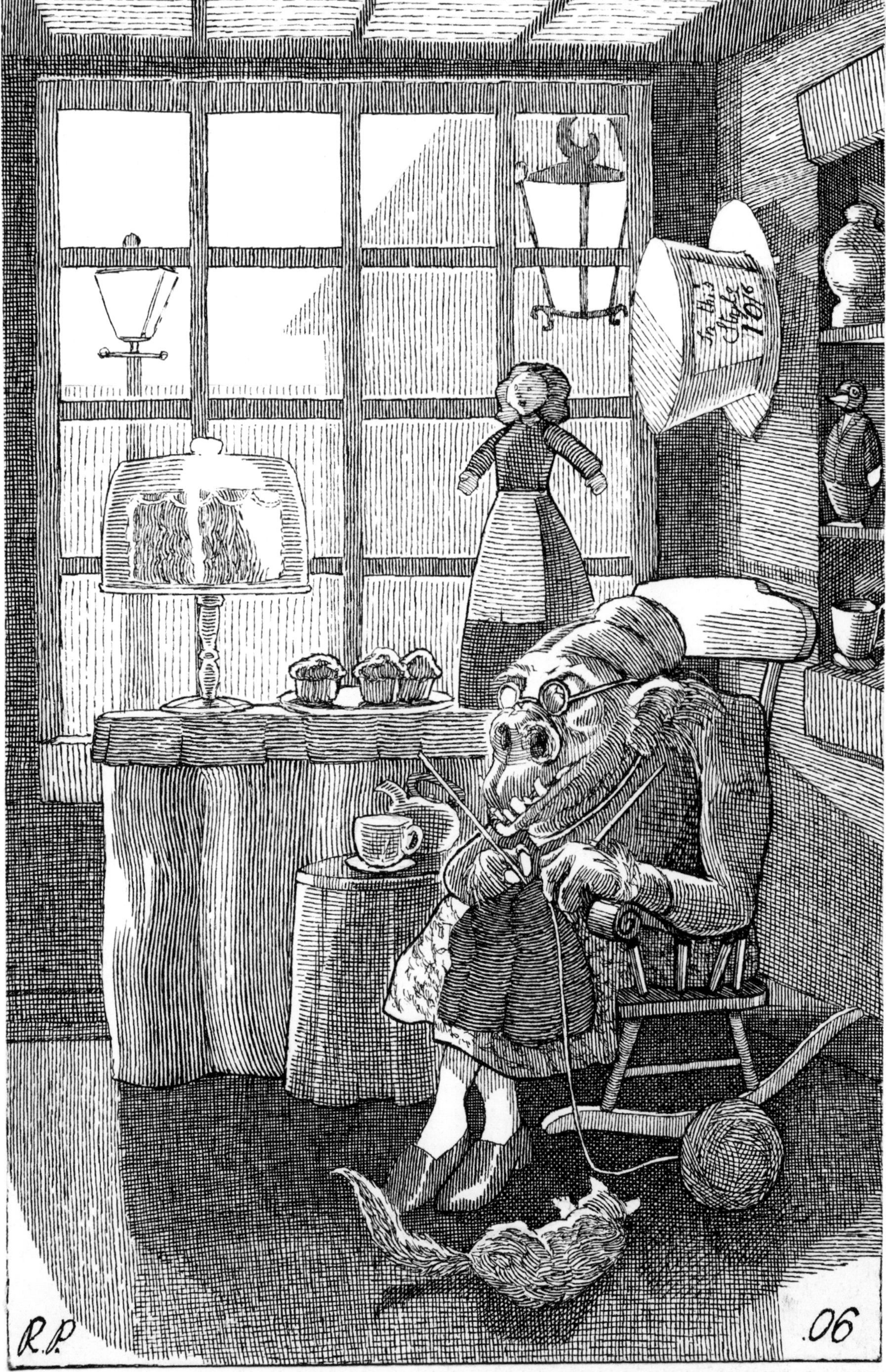
In this Style 10/6
R.P.
.06

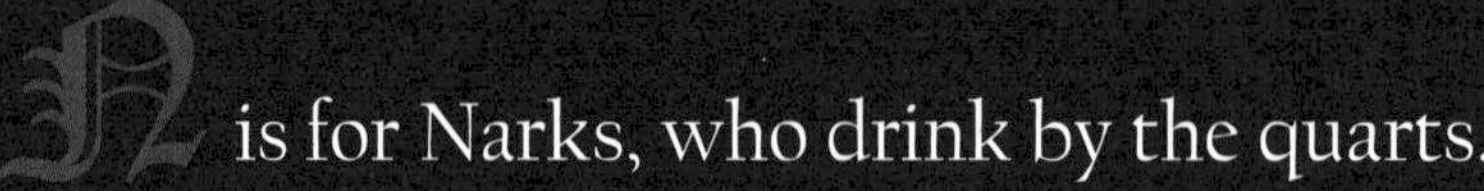

N is for Narks, who drink by the quarts.

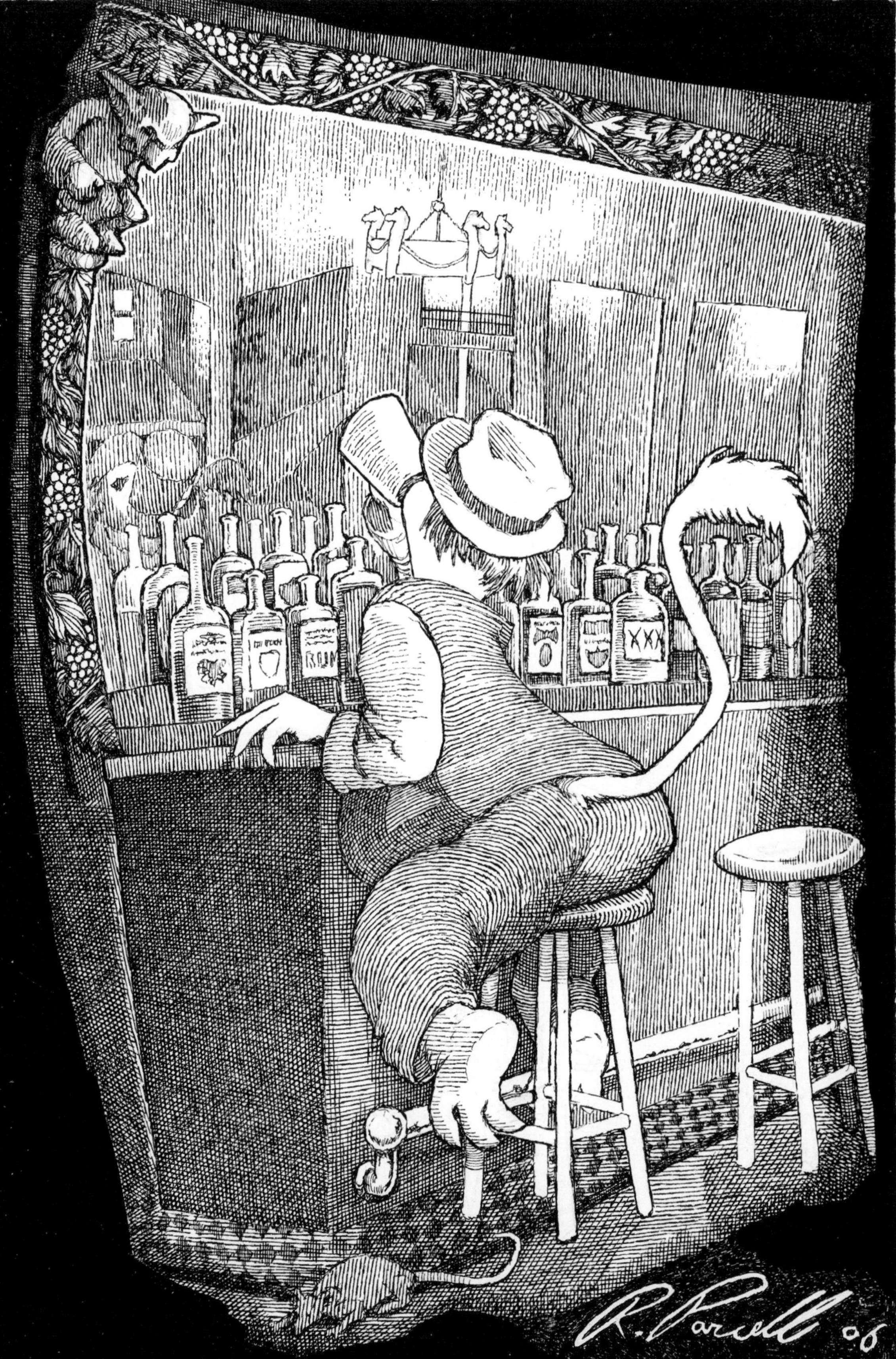
RUM
XXX

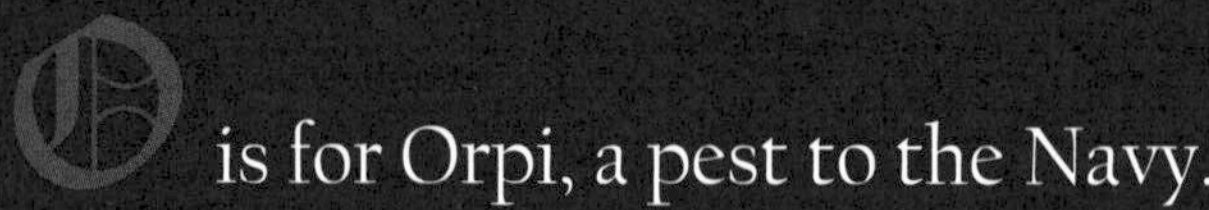

O is for Orpi, a pest to the Navy.

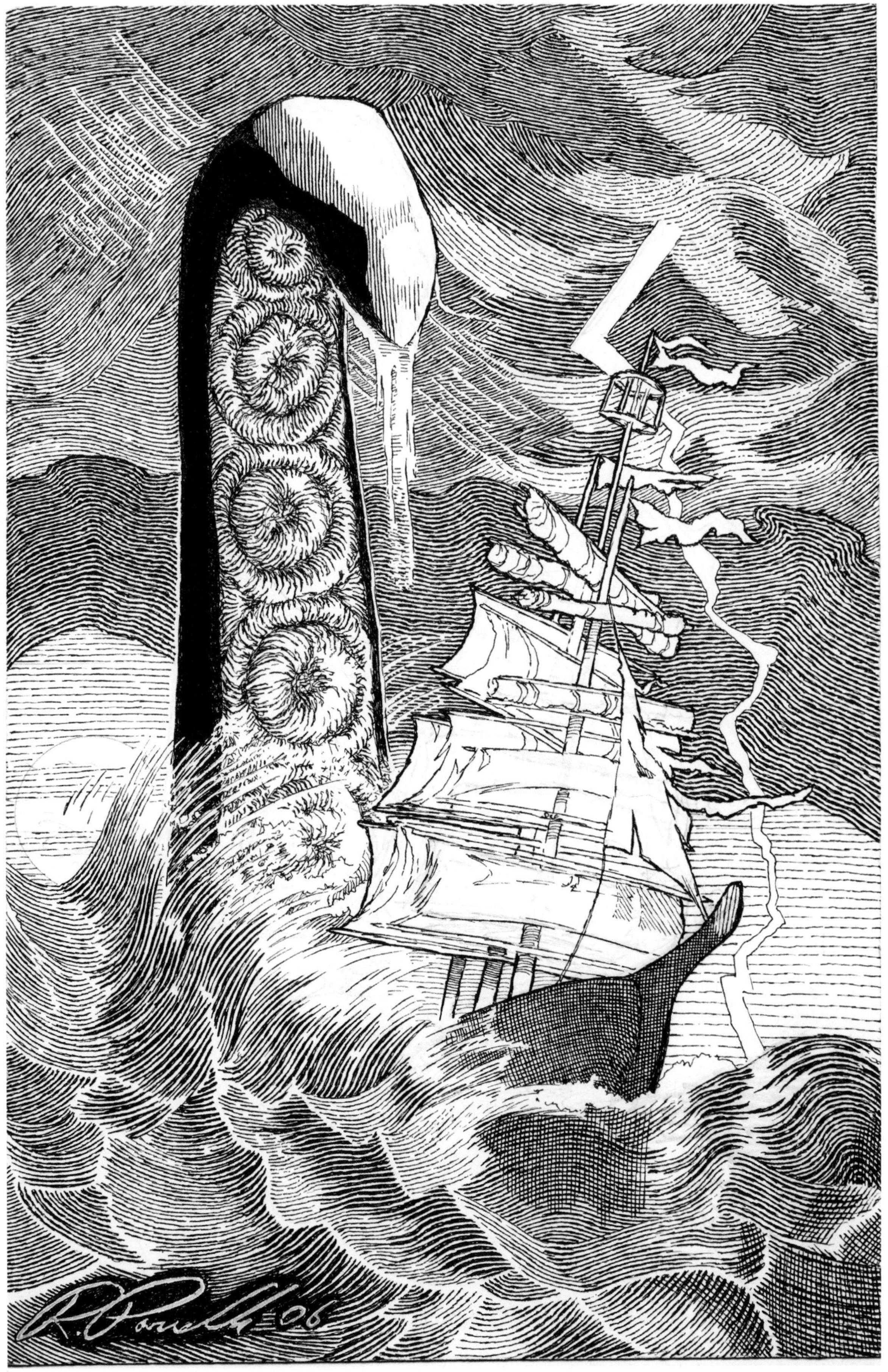

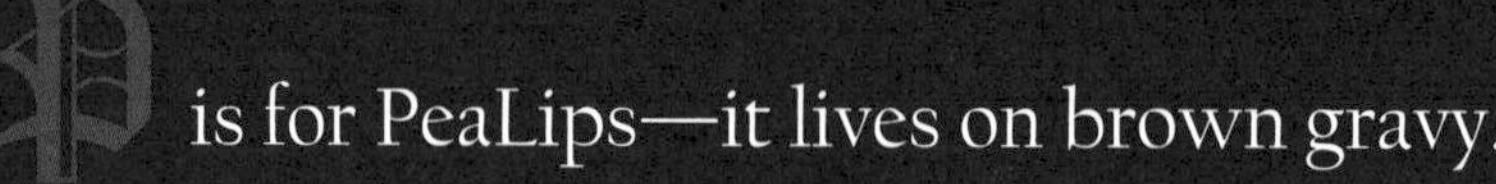

P is for PeaLips—it lives on brown gravy.

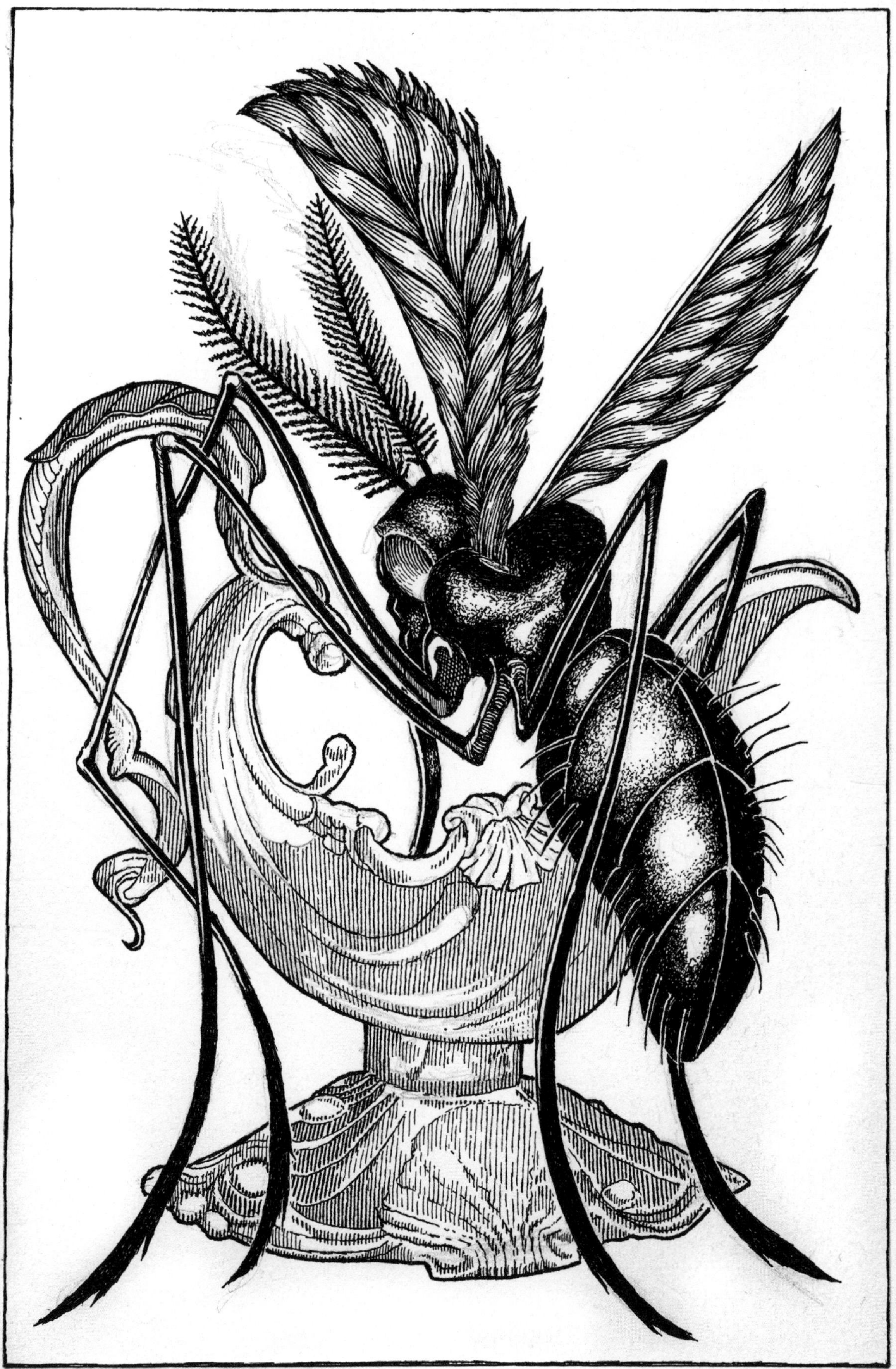

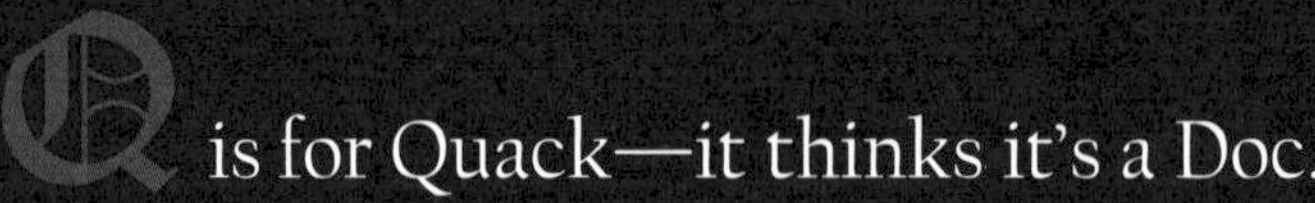
Q is for Quack—it thinks it's a Doc.

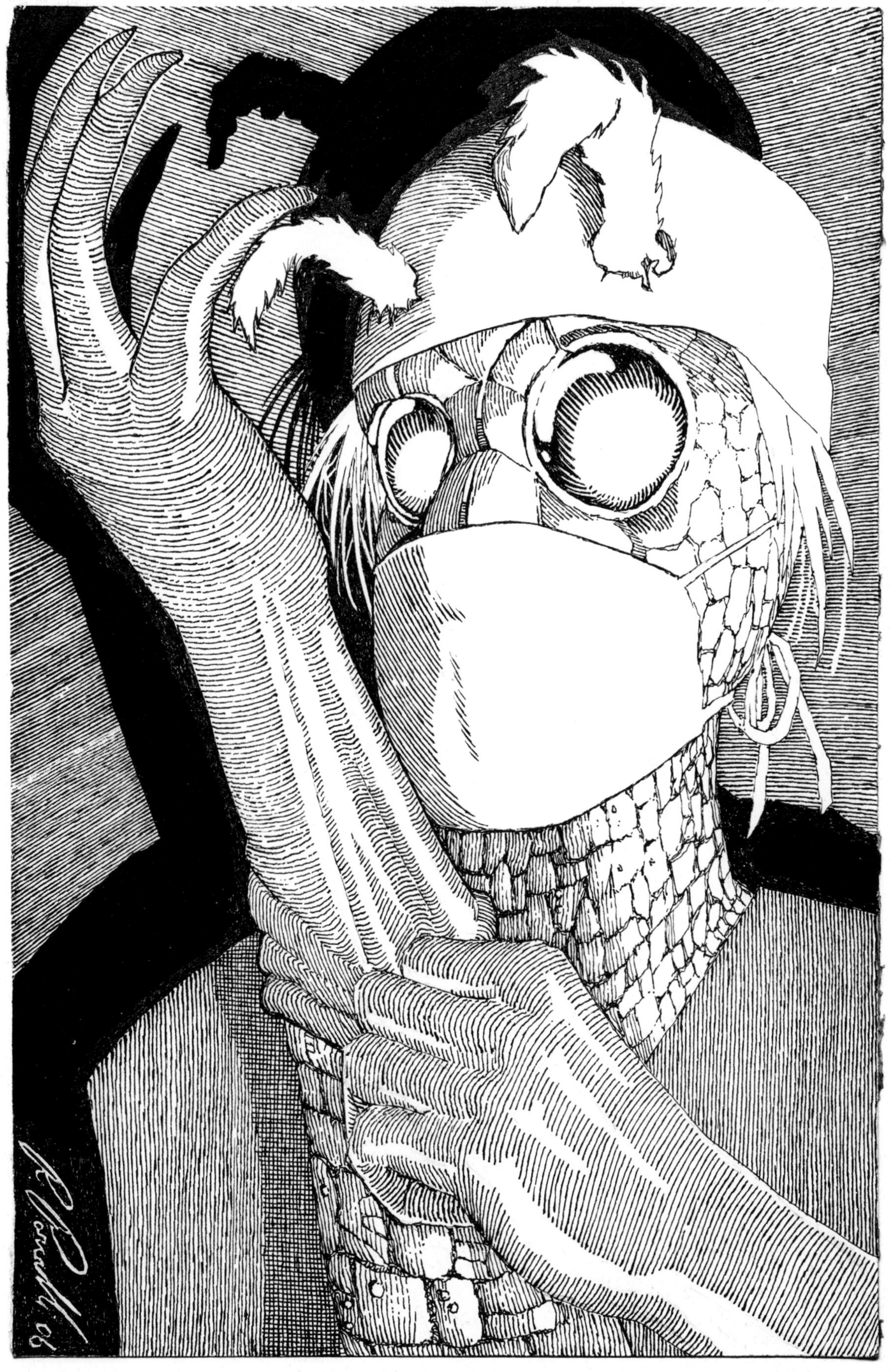

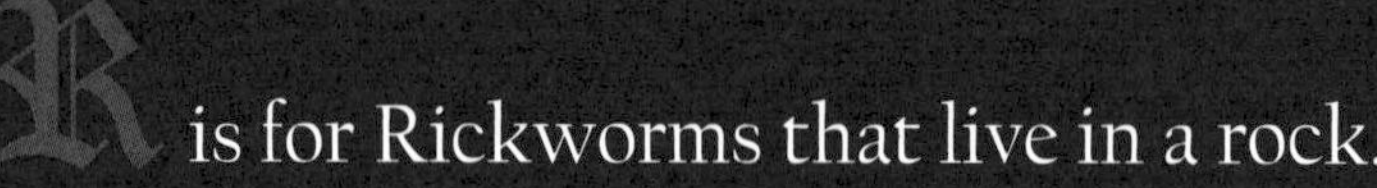

R is for Rickworms that live in a rock.

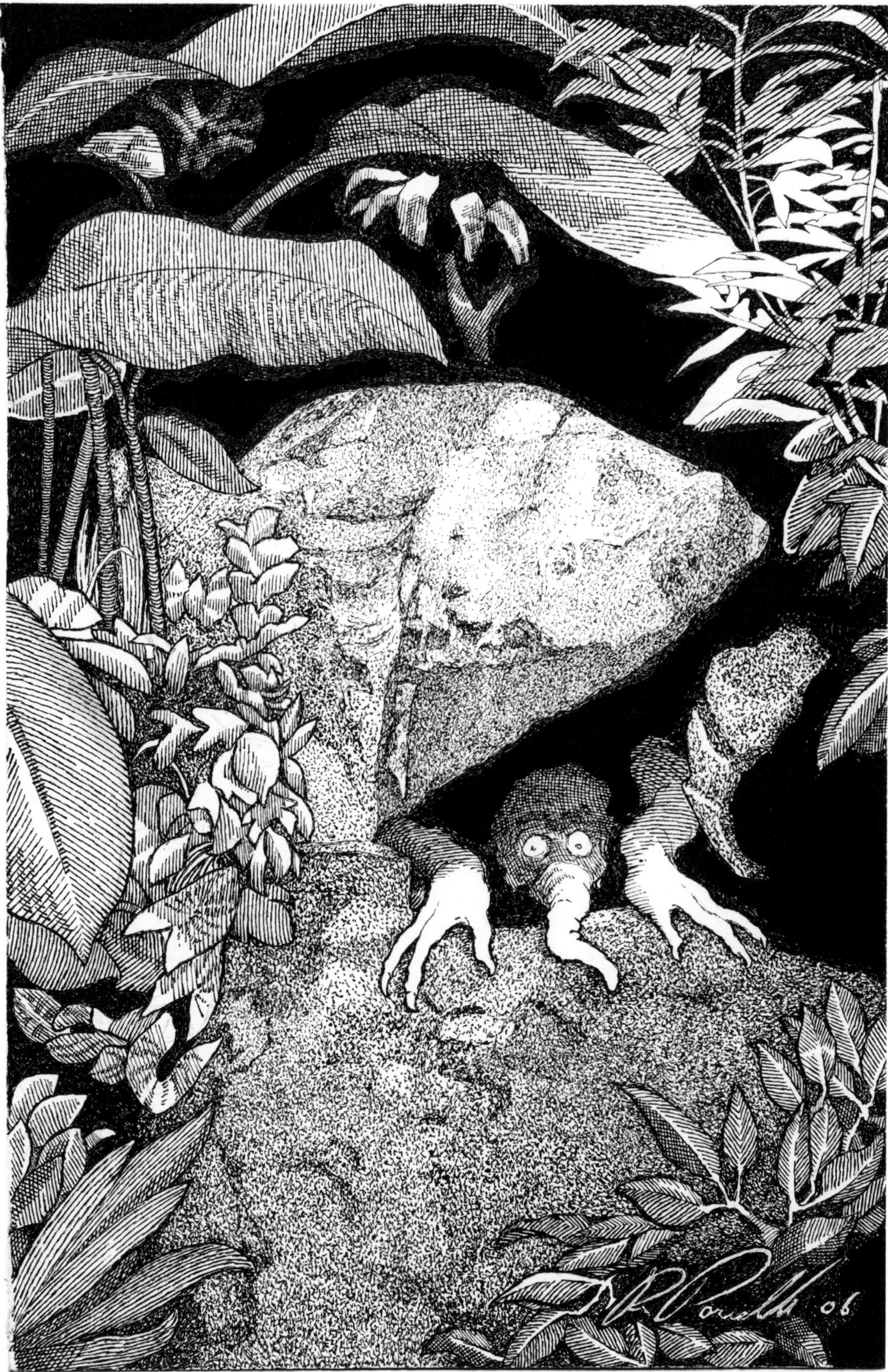

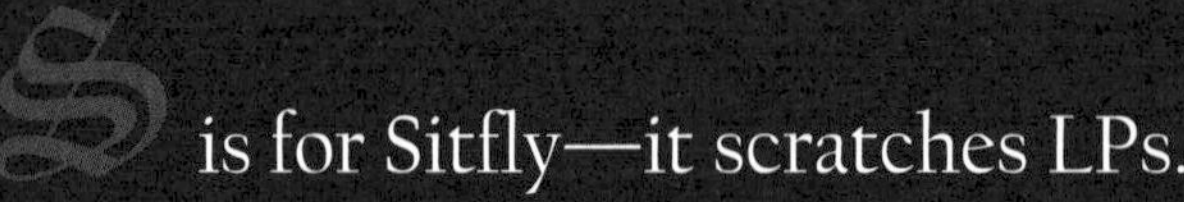
S is for Sitfly—it scratches LPs.

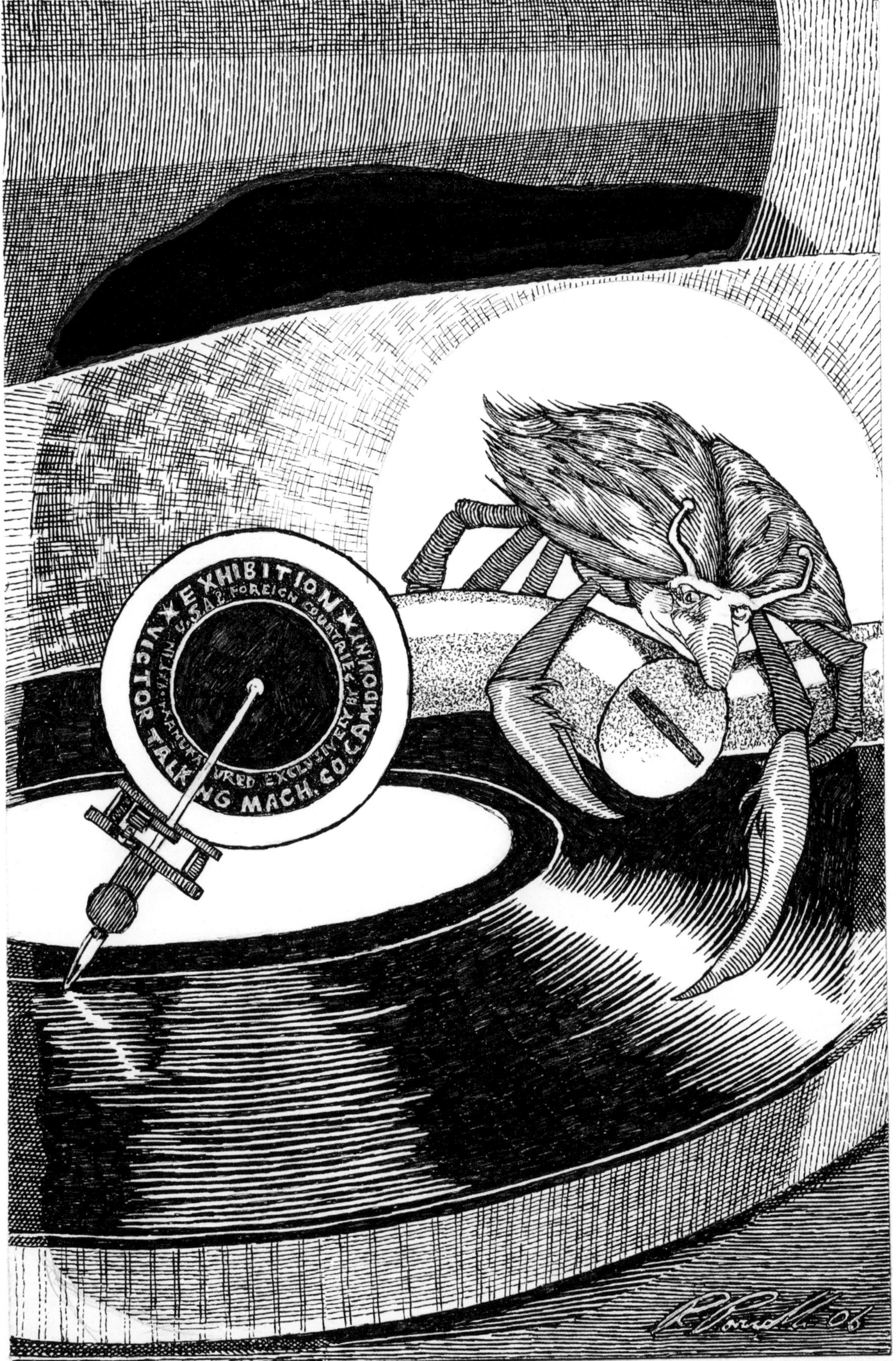
EXHIBITION
U.S.A. & FOREIGN COUNTRIES
MANUFACTURED EXCLUSIVELY BY
VICTOR TALKING MACH. CO.

T is for Titmoose—it walks on its knees.

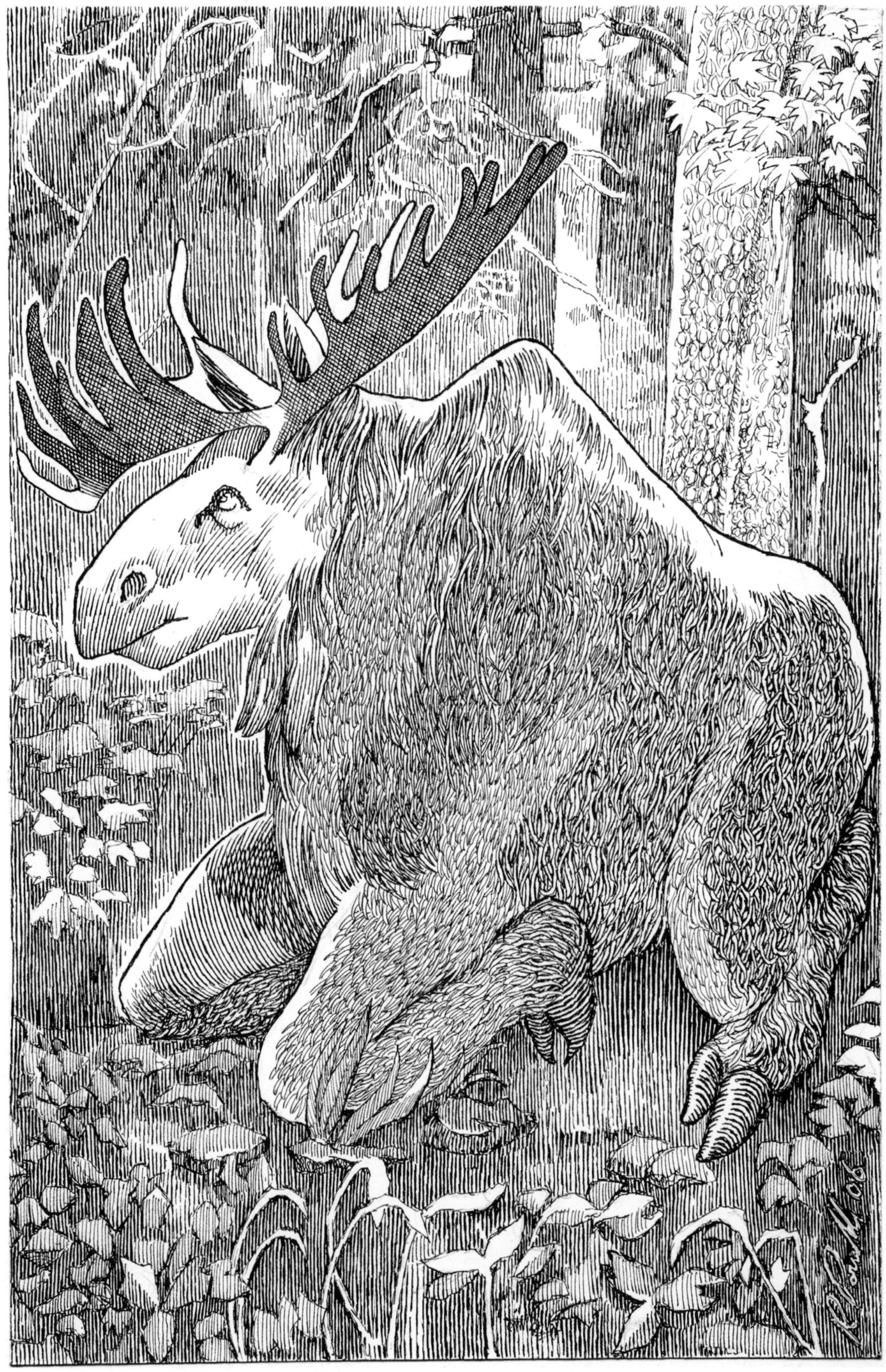

U is for Uttlies, kind but don't show it.

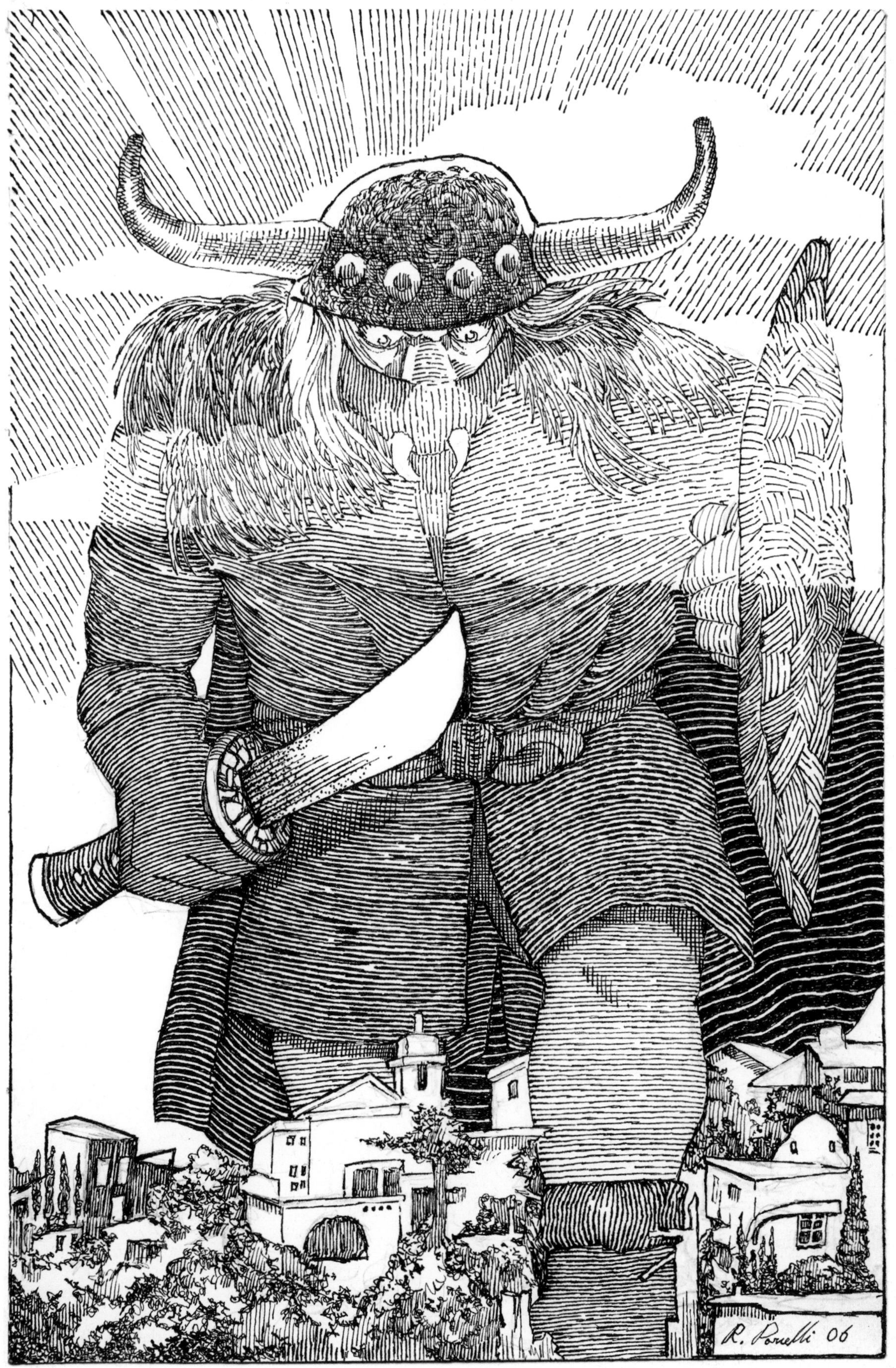

V is for Vanishsaurs, extinct but don't know it.

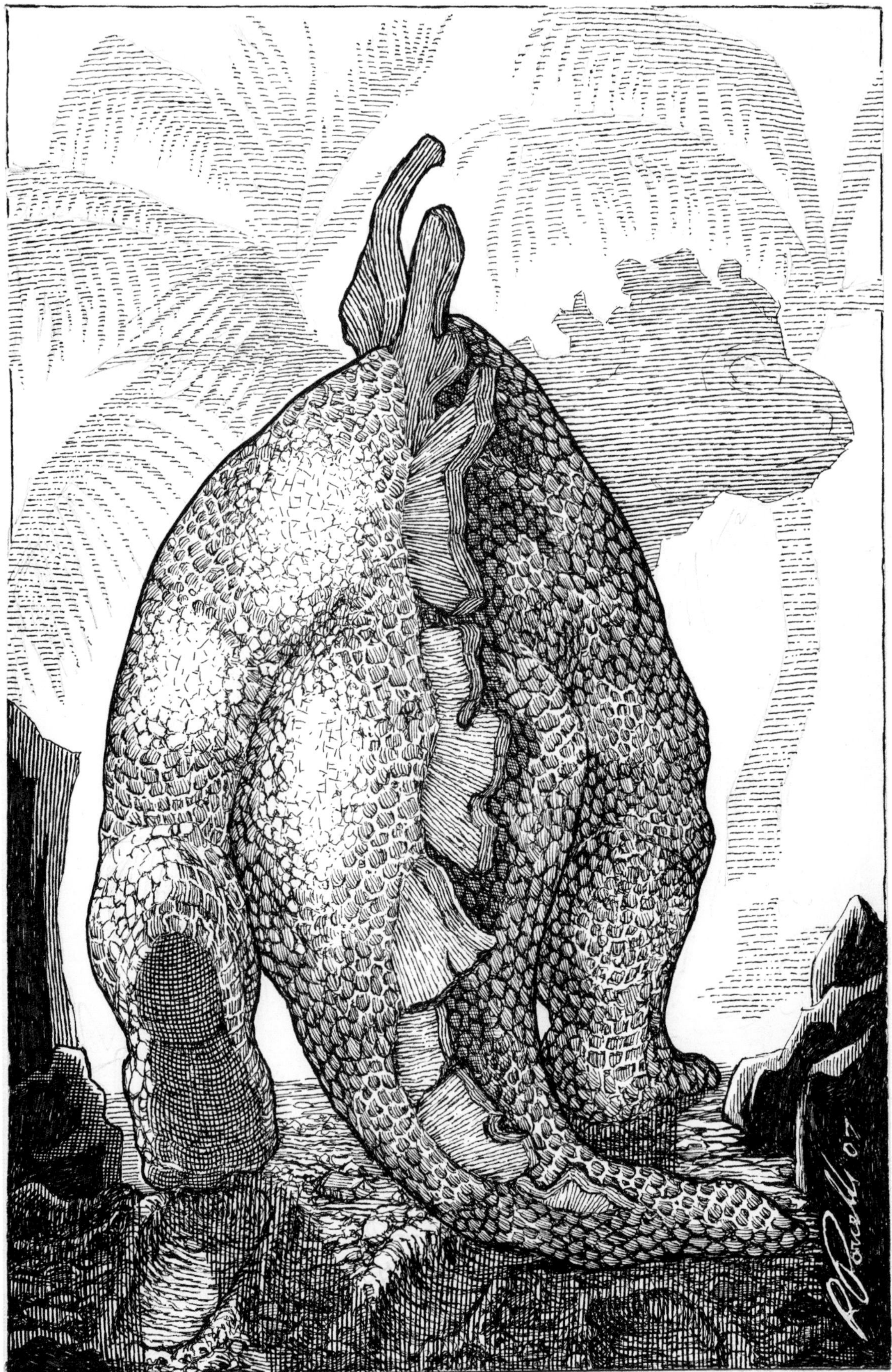

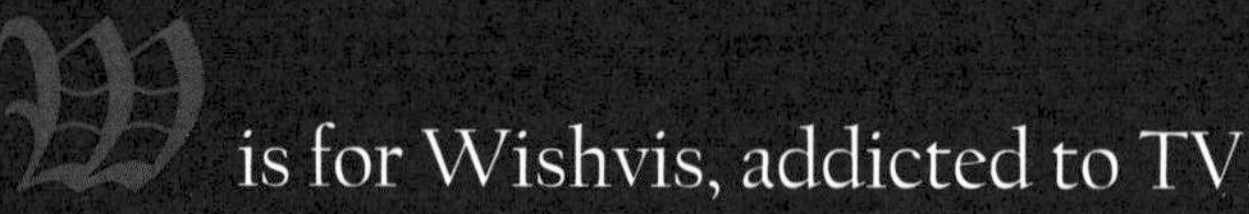

W is for Wishvis, addicted to TV.

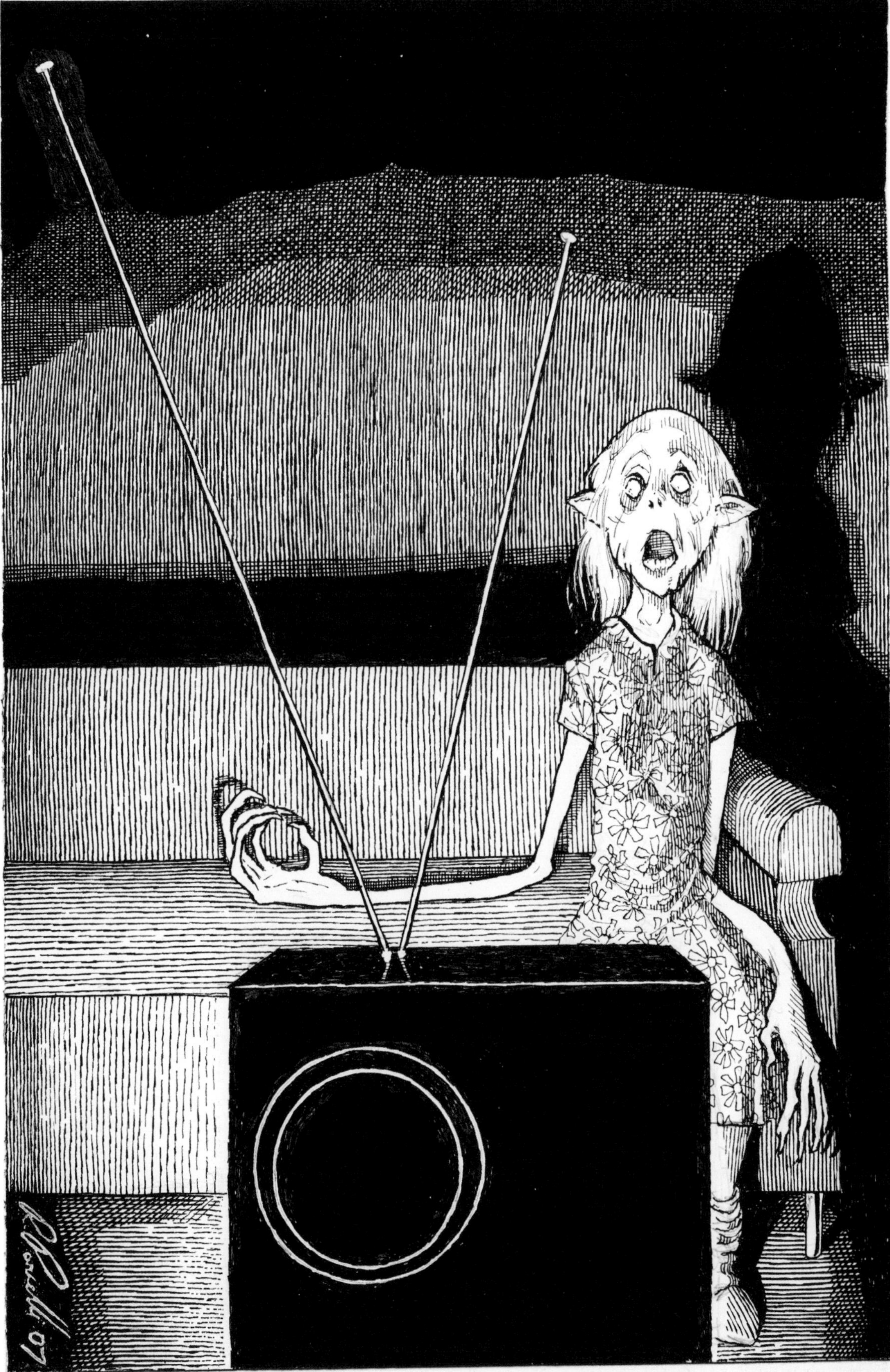

X is for XyLong—it stings like a bee.

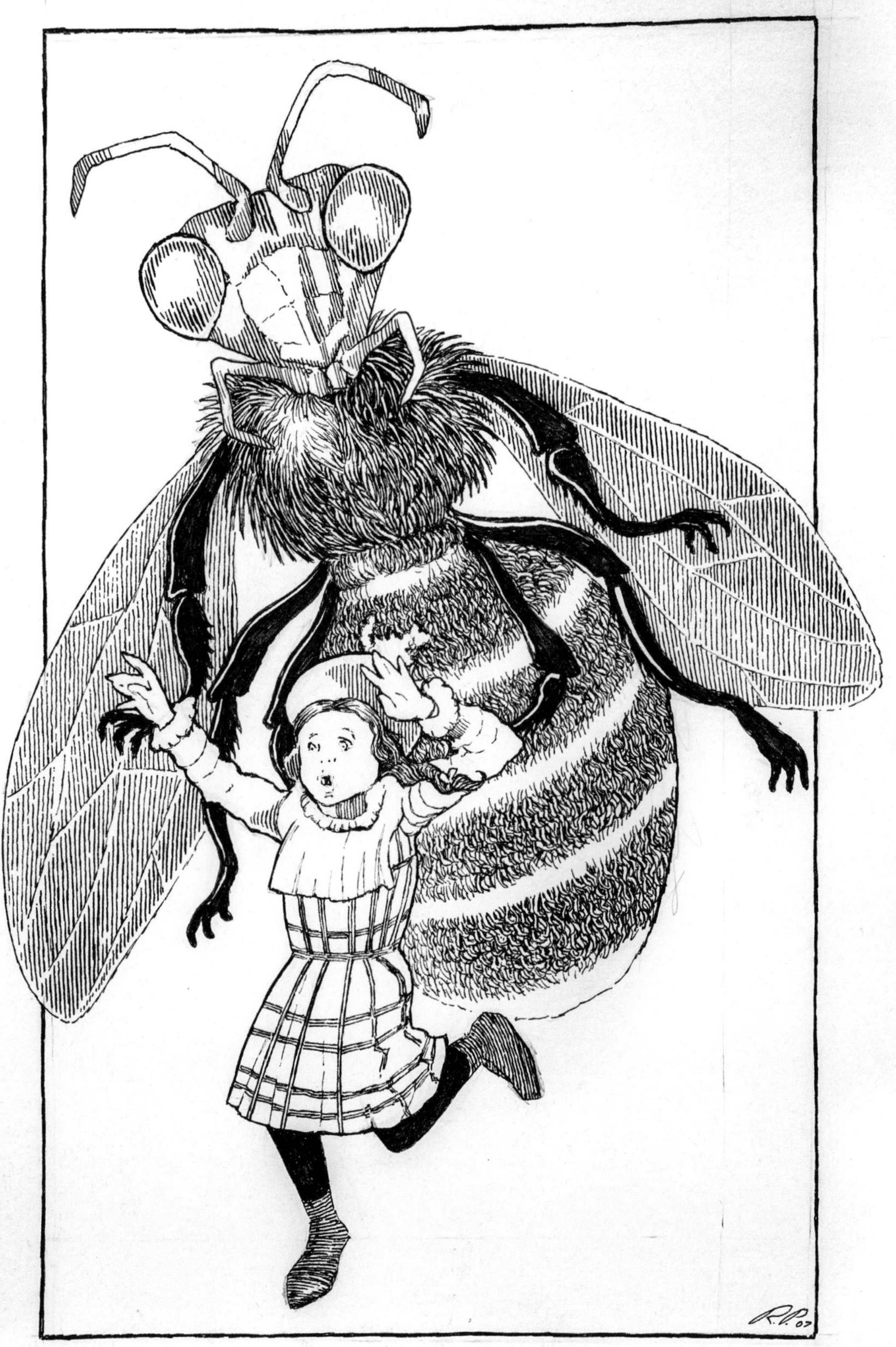

Yellowfly is a creature that starts with a Y.

It uses its wings, but never to fly.

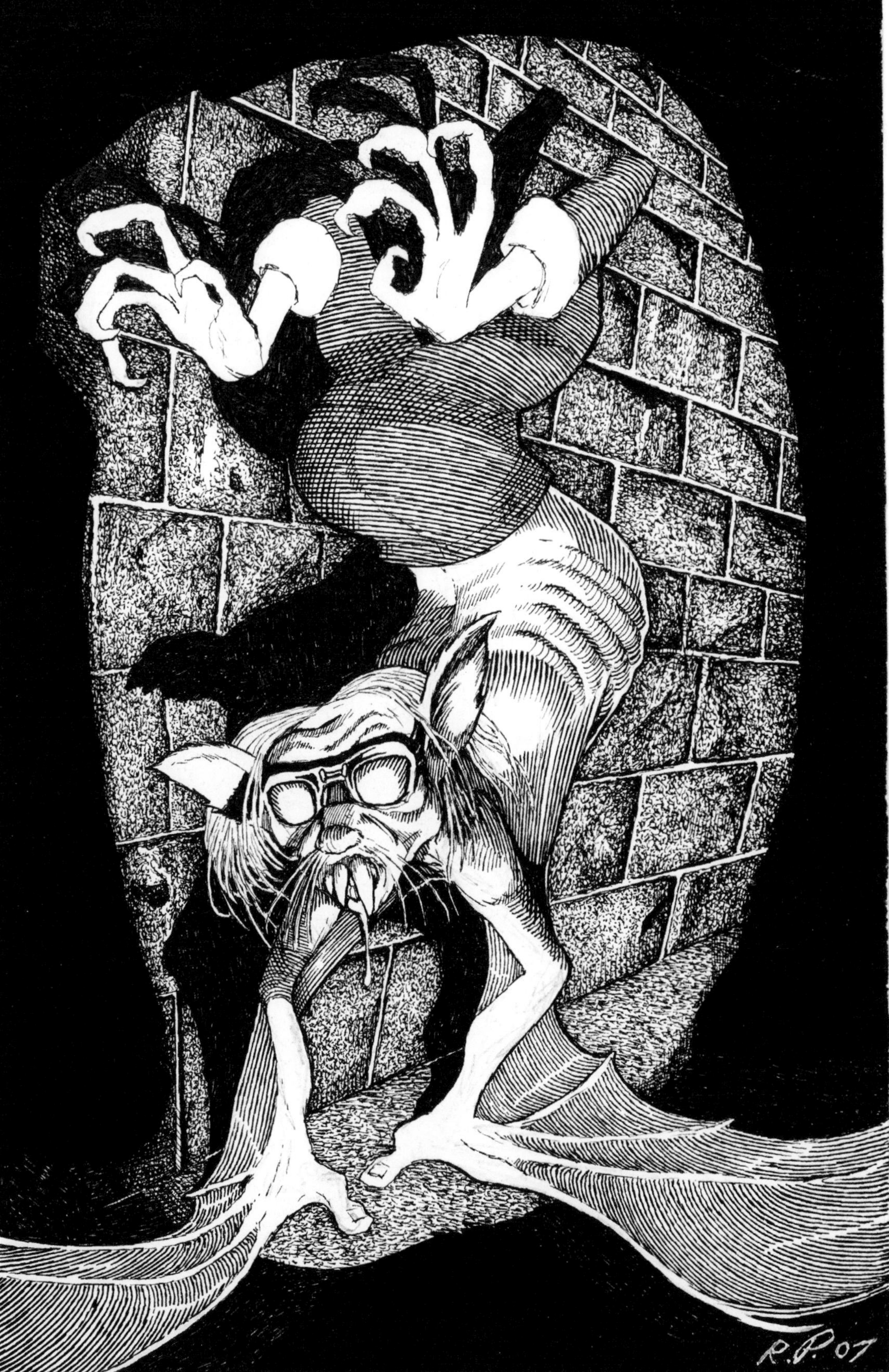
R.P. 07

And last of all Zookins: it starts with a Z.

They're big and they're hairy, unpleasant to see.

But last it is and last it will be—

Thus ends this strange, macabre literati.

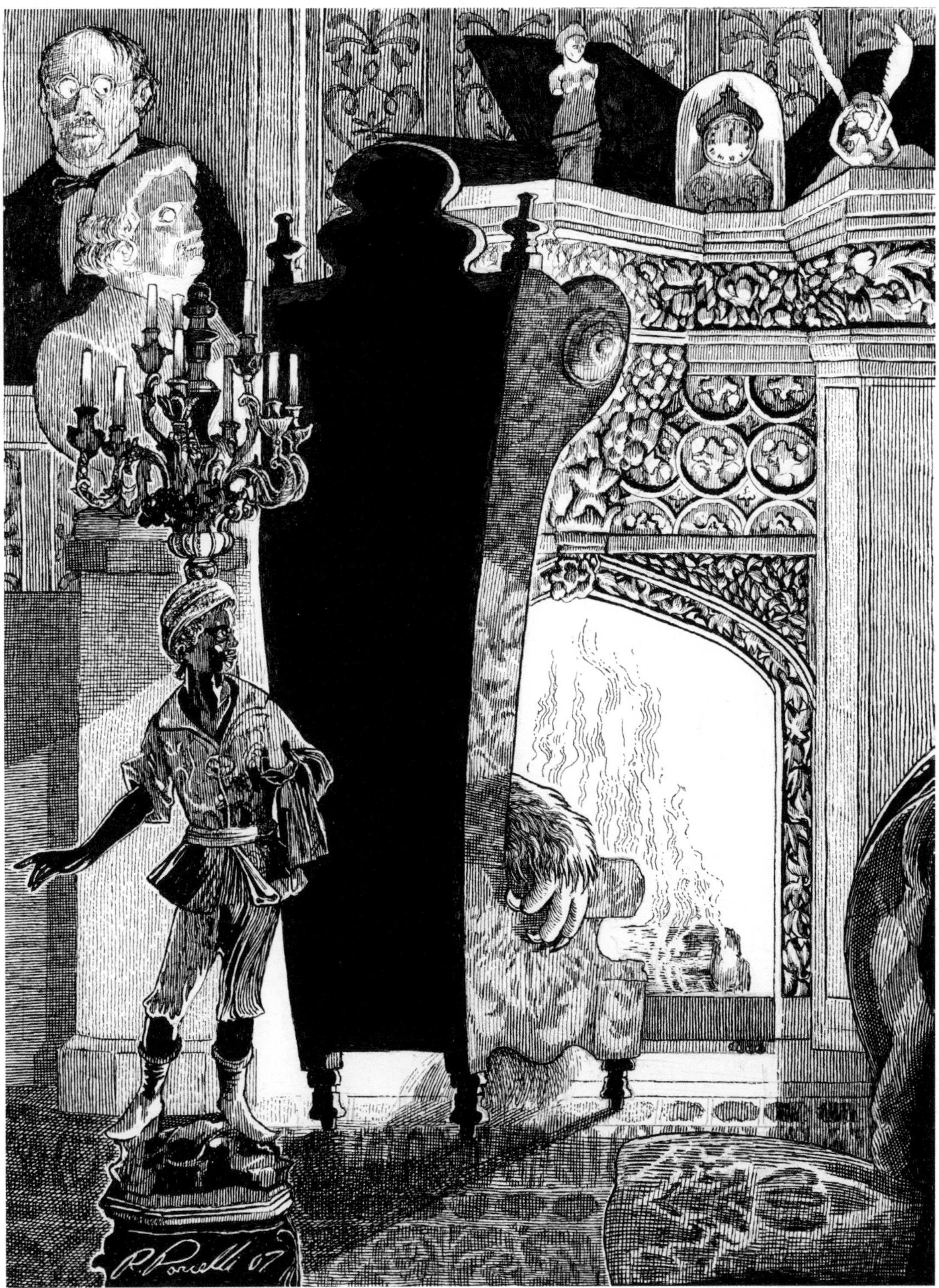

a Closing Prayer

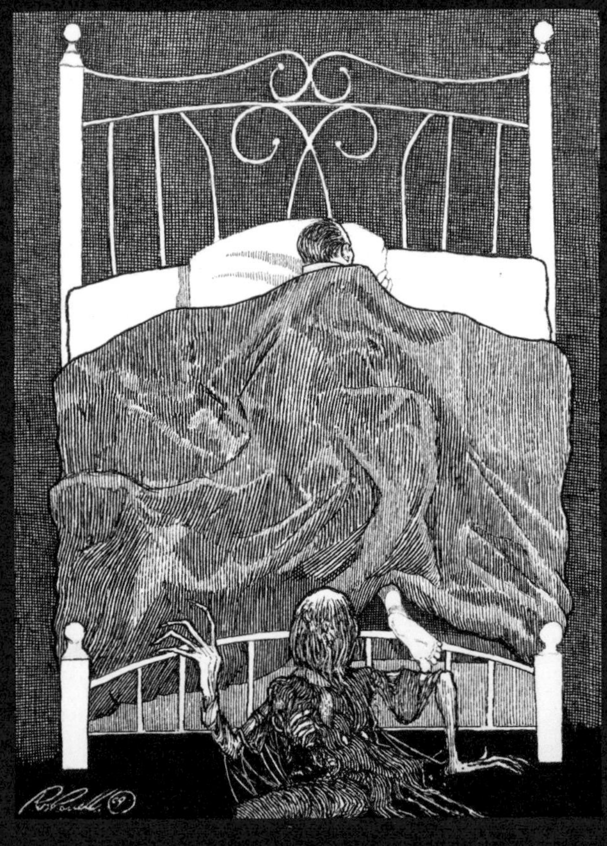

From ghoulies

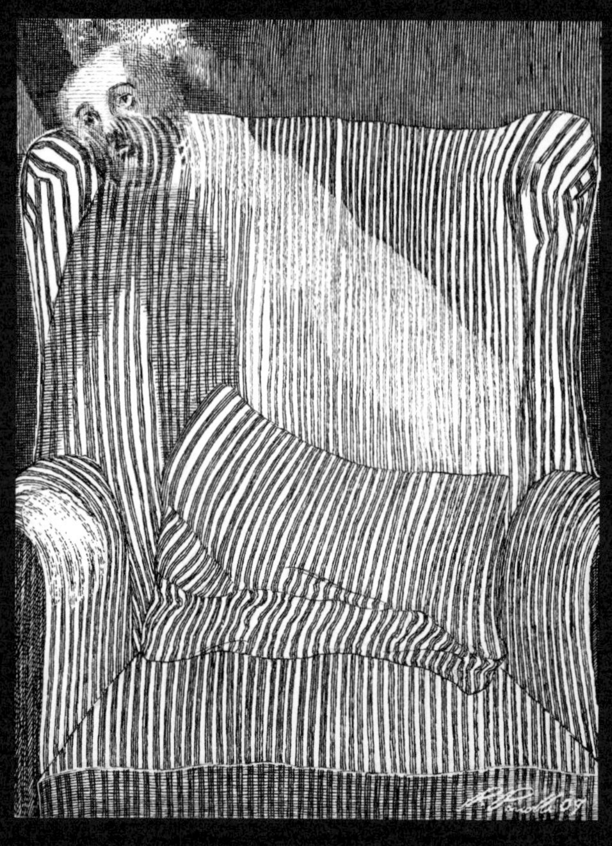

and ghosties

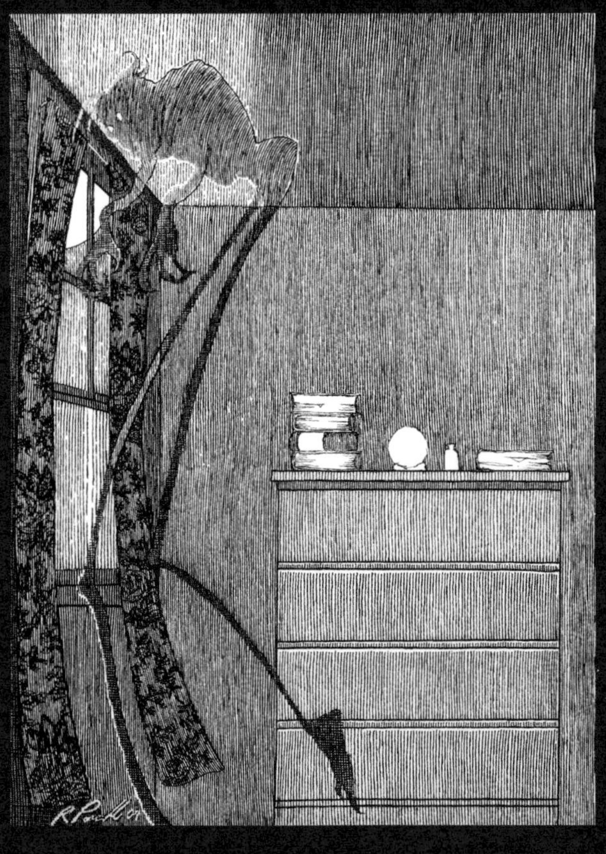

And long-leggedy beasties

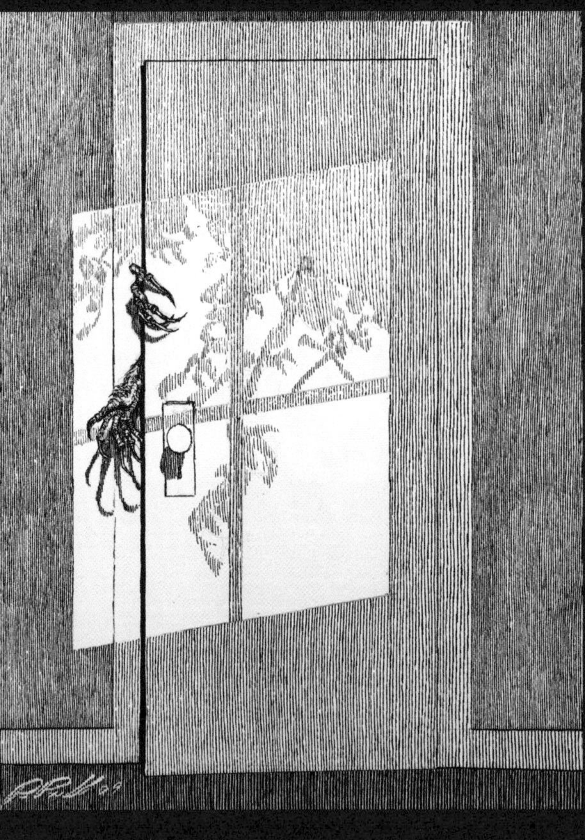

And things that go bump in the night,

Good Lord, deliver us!

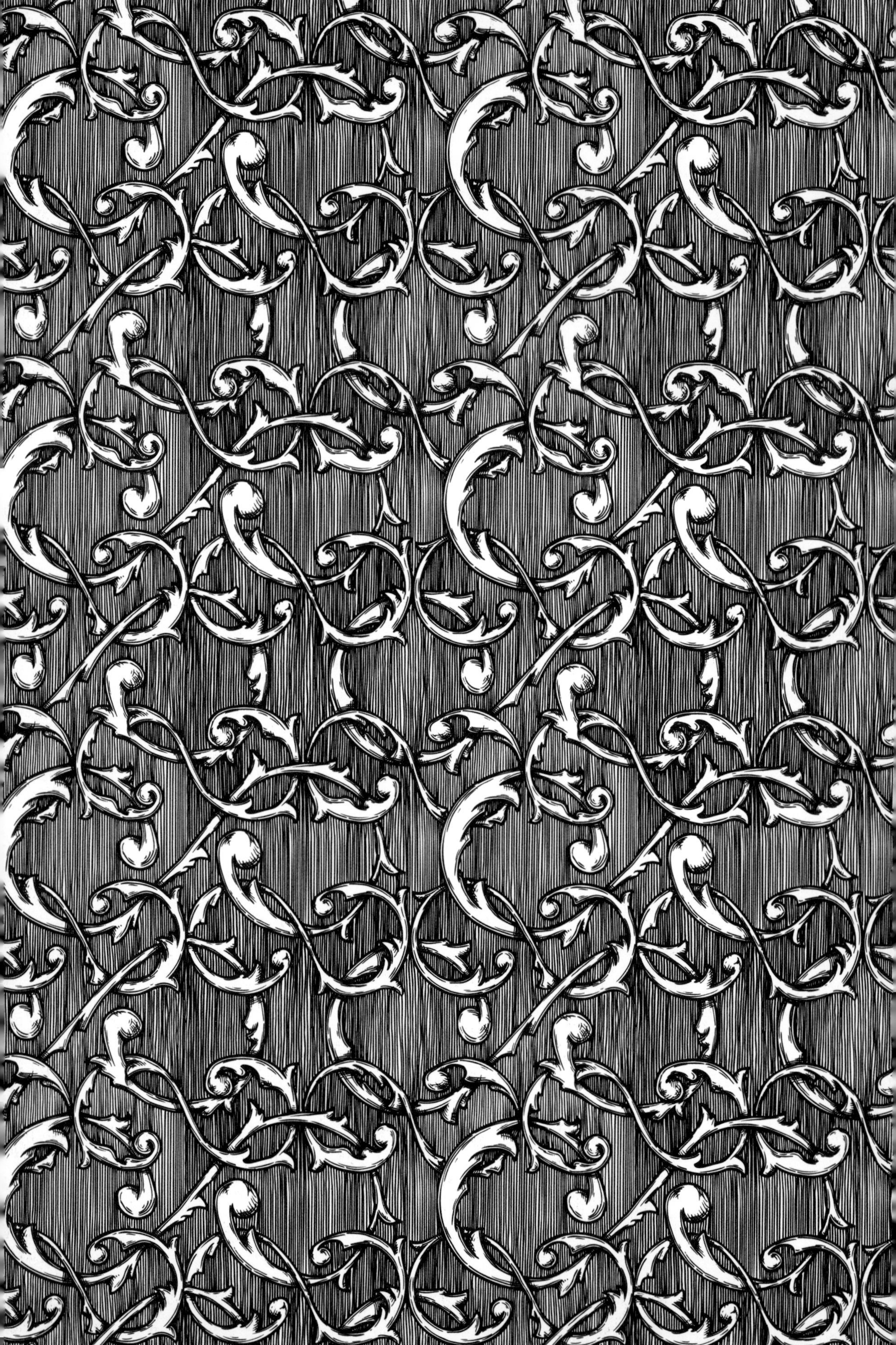